Business Ownership Mindset

The ultimate guide to freedom and self-expression through building a seven figure business.

Michelle Nedelec

Business Ownership Mindset

© 2017 Awareness Strategies Inc.

Jacket photograph credit Sid Helischauer

© Michelle Nedelec

All rights reserved. Without limiting the rights under copyright reserved above, no part of this publication may be reproduced, stored in or introduced into a retrieval system, or transmitted in any form or by any means (electronic, mechanical, photocopying, recording or otherwise), without the prior written permission of the copyright owner of this book.

www.BusinessOwnershipMindset.com

www.AwarenessStrategies.com

www.MichelleNedelec.com

www.SuccessTherapy.ca

ISBN-13: 978-1542979474
ISBN-10: 1542979471

Business Ownership Mindset

This book is designed to help people who are ready for the next stage in their business evolution. We all enter the business evolution in some capacity. We start off as a consumer and that may be all we ever do. Some people move on and get a job, whether it's delivering papers or working at a fast food chain. We become employees. We may progress down the employee trail or up the corporate ladder; even all the way up to CEO. At some point, some people decide to go into sales and some decide to run their own companies. From there, they evolve into a Business Ownership Mindset; the ultimate form of freedom and self-expression. But know this; the rules of the game are different at every level. And to pass through each level you will have to evolve and change your way of thinking, believing and acting. Warning: Failure to evolve through each mindset is a recipe for failure.

Business Ownership Mindset

Contents

Chapter 1 The Evolution of Thought through Business... 9

1. Progression from Consumer to BOM 9
2. Consumer.. 11
3. Employee 14
4. Sales 19
5. Management 22
6. Entrepreneur 25
7. Business Ownership Mindset 27
8. In Conclusion 29

Chapter 2 Business as a form of Self-Expression........... 31

1. The type of business we choose 33
2. The way we deal with others.................................... 35
3. The value we feel we bring to the table. 40
4. The "problem" we have that's to be solved.............. 45

Chapter 3 Self-Actualization and the importance of it. 50

1. Maslow's hierarchy and the flipside of it. 50
2. What is Self-Actualization?....................................... 54
3. How do we self-actualize?.. 57

Chapter 4 Enlightenment through Business.................. 61

1. It brings up our resistance. 61
2. What is resistance?.. 63
3. How does Resistance show up? 65
4. How do we let go of it?.. 67

Business Ownership Mindset

    5.   How it happens; an evolutionary process 72

    6.   For the good of all mankind or just the shareholders ... 74

    7.   Business is the best personal development training 77

Chapter 5 Rules of the game as employee through to BOM And why they aren't transferable 79

    1.   Succeeding as an Employee 82

    2.   Succeeding as a Sales Rep 83

    3.   Succeeding as a Manager 84

    4.   Succeeding as an Entrepreneur 85

    5.   Succeeding as a Business Owner 87

Chapter 6 How to fail in Business (Don't evolve, stay the same) 90

    1.   Other people's needs are more important. 90

    2.   Caring what other people think; judgement. 92

    3.   Self-Doubt 93

    4.   Know it all 96

Chapter 7 How to Succeed as a Business Owner 99

    1.   Know what you want and go after it. 99

    2.   Reverse engineer your plan. 101

    3.   Strategize 103

    4.   Ask for what you want, especially help 104

    5.   What most people think failure is and why it is essential to success. 106

Chapter 8 The importance of a vision 108

    1.   Being a Visionary. 108

Business Ownership Mindset

    2.   Reverse engineer vs buildout. 110

Chapter 9 Creating a Vision 111

    1.   The Process 111

        a.   Business Plan 111

        b.   What problem do you solve for your client? 118

        c.   Where do you fit in the market? 120

        d.   Who is your ideal client? 122

        e.   What is your brand/reputation? 124

        f.   What projects do you want to take on? 125

    2.   Reverse Engineering it. 126

        a.   Starting with the end goal in mind 126

        b.   What people do you need on your team and when? 127

        c.   What systems do you need/when? 128

        d.   How do you want to get it to market/marketing? .. 130

    3.   Strategy for implementation. 131

    4.   Overcoming Obstacles. 134

    5.   Leadership Mindset 136

Chapter 10 The importance of honouring your Choices 138

    1.   It's the only way to get things done. 138

    2.   Your logical mind knows the plan 140

    3.   Your emotional spontaneous mind and sabotage 144

Chapter 11 How to Honour Your Choices 145

    1.   Time Blocking 145

Business Ownership Mindset

    2. Micro Time Blocking 146

    3. Beliefs Around Time Blocking - how to engage your whole body. 147

    4. Now Go Do it. 149

Chapter 12   The Importance of Language and Your Self Talk 151

    1. You are your Head Cheerleader 151

    2. The Path of Least Resistance 153

    3. Now Go Do it. 154

Chapter 13 Creating a Philosophy that works for you 155

    1. Social Acceptance (Political Correctness and why it'll be the death of you) 155

    2. Multiple ways to think successfully. 164

    3. Figuring out what's important for you. 166

    4. Tools and Tricks 168

    5. Now Go Do it. 169

Chapter 14 Strategy vs Tactics 171

    1. Big Picture, little picture, what begins with a picture? 171

    2. Strategical Thinking and Tactical Thinking 175

    3. Why you need to be thinking Strategically 176

    4. Pay Grade appropriate Strategizing 177

Chapter 15 How to Strategize 178

    1. Setting up time to do it; NGDI 178

    2. What to do in that time; NGDI 179

    3. Allocating Tasks; NGDI 181

Business Ownership Mindset

  4. Accountability; NGDI 183

Chapter 16 Support 186

  1. Setting up a team... 186

  2. Masterminding 189

  3. Letting Go of Resistance 190

  4. Coaching 193

Chapter 17 Conclusion... 195

  1. Review Highlights 195

  2. Now Go Do it 196

  3. Come Back in a Month and Do it Again. 197

  The hypothesis of a thesis 198

Business Ownership Mindset

Chapter 1
The Evolution of Thought through Business

1. **Progression from Consumer to BOM**

In life, we all start off completely dependent on others to have our basic needs met. As we grow up, we learn that we need things in order to survive. Whether we get those things from the land or a shopping mall is irrelevant to us at that time. We simply know that we need food to survive, and shelter to support us. As such, to one extent or another, we are consumers.

Somewhere along the journey some of us realize that we want to, or in some circumstances have to, get money coming in to pay for those items. Where we start in the job market varies. Some people start off getting a job in their family's business or the fast food joint down the street. Some people go into sales, whether they know it or not, by selling newspapers or selling cookies. And, then there are the born entrepreneurs who have it figured out from an early age and get lawn mowing jobs from the neighbours and then pay their friends do the work.

Regardless of where we start our working careers there is a definite echelon to the thought process even though it's very rarely navigated in an orderly fashion. How we navigate from consumer to wherever we end up is a matter of personal nurture and nature's influences. The purpose of this book is to begin to unravel the mystery of what it takes to get from one level to the next successfully and as quickly as you would like.

Contrary to popular perception, the progression is not simply a growth of scope of knowledge. It's not simply learning new tactics and

Business Ownership Mindset

knowing WHAT to do. It's an evolution of thought and self-discovery. We cannot go through these levels without greater self-knowledge and understanding.

Now, not everyone wants to transition from one to the next and some people find themselves on track to go from one to the next whether they "want" to or not. I believe everything is a choice, but sometimes we make choices we don't want for the benefits we receive, no matter how convoluted they may be.

As I see it, having worked with thousands of people, there are definite transitions in thinking from a consumer to an employee, from an employee to a sales role, from sales to management, from management to entrepreneurship and from entrepreneurship into business ownership.

I know that there are millions of ways of navigating the workplace from consumer to death and rarely do two people ever cover the same path. If, however, we look at the skill sets that build one level to the next we can see that in an ideal world we can transition from one position to the next without being overwhelmed, lost and quite frankly feeling completely incompetent. In fact, we can master a certain skill set and move into a new position taking with us the acquired skills and build on them in a healthy and productive manner.

The confusion begins when the skills and mindset required for one position are completely opposite and in opposition to the skills and mindset required for the next position. How do you know what to hold on to and master, and what to let go of and forget?

Business Ownership Mindset

2. <u>Consumer</u>

The consumer level can be a very easy level for us to master. Most of us have it mastered before we can walk. We want something, we ask for it, we get it, we consume it, and we wait until we need or want something again. Some might call it a childhood innocence when we're in need or want of something and it is provided to us. Consumer might not be the best title for this, but you'll get the idea.

The issue with mastering this skill at such a young age is that it tends to give us a false sense of satisfaction more often than not. This is, for the most part, why North Americans tend to be over the top consumers even though they've transitioned into other levels of the work place. If their day doesn't go as anticipated they can always fall back on a skill they've mastered, head over to the store and buy something and "voila!" they have a sense of satisfaction knowing that they've done something well.

By not understanding that humans get their sense of satisfaction from accomplishment, contribution, and self-expression, these consumers look solely to something superficial and within their current level of mastery and do it over and over again like a hamster in a scientist's machine getting their nugget of "something" and an electric jolt to their neural happy place. The same thing happens with any addiction really, but I'll stick to focusing on occupational transformations here.

The process of asking for what we want and getting it is the foundation to all occupation. Regardless of the current monetary system and using it as a transitional piece from knowing what you want, to getting what you want, the system of offering services in return for goods received is primordial. It is as basic and fundamental to our existence as sleep.

Even the babe in swaddling cloth is offering a service in return for

Business Ownership Mindset

the goods it receives. Ask any parent who feeds their child. There is a definite perceived value, whether it's someone to simply hold, or someone to accept their love and care. There is a definite value in simply the existence of that child that warrants the delivery of the goods asked for whether it's food, shelter, warmth, or otherwise. And if you don't believe it, ask any parent who abandons and doesn't feed their child.

This brings on a whole new issue for that child if they buy into the idea that they don't have that value, just because someone else failed to notice or acknowledge it. Unfortunately most of us buy into that idea to some extent, which is why many go into the work force in the first place and why many of us flail around trying to find out where we fit, what we're good at, and what we like. We think we "have to" do what we're told to do and to some extent that we have no value until we develop skills.

There are some people who choose to not enter the work force their entire lives and there is absolutely nothing wrong with that. Actually, it can be delightful! There are many ways to accomplish tasks, to contribute and self-express without entering the work force. With our current monetary system, the majority of people in North America opt into working in the occupational system because it seems easier to get what they want, having more freedom to decide where the payment comes from and where the goods are purchased. Or as I mentioned before, they don't realize that they are valuable and can get what they want without having to become more skilled; "better."

There is a definite mindset that allows one to master consumerism. It requires knowing your value and having the tenacity to go after what you want. The majority of people are not in that state of mind, so they do what they're told and they go out and "get a good job." (whatever that might mean).

There are people outside of the workforce who are not masters of

Business Ownership Mindset

consumerism, people who want to get a job but cannot hold one down. These people are not the masters of this field by any sort. They do not know who they are, they do not know what they want or how to get it, and they are unfortunately misplaced from the system and unable to fit in any of the positions. With a little work on their inner game, some of them can become stellar, but it requires knowing "who they are" and the willingness to let go of preconceived notions of what success is in their minds. It sounds ironic, I know. That's because it is ironic. People, who get fired from their jobs for having bad attitudes, or poor attendance, are for the most part, trying to fit a square peg into a round hole. They likely have very spirited and creative mindsets but they get jobs that are detail oriented and repetitive because they're told that's what they should do. Or they're great a seeing the big picture, but they're not willing to put in the time to either collect the money or the experience they need to in order to run the show. These individuals have "failed" in the workforce because they don't know "who they are" and they're trying to buy into someone else's set of rules. We'll talk a lot more about this in the chapter on how to fail in business because I'm sure you'll agree that it's important to know how to side step this obstacle so that it doesn't affect you.

So let's assume that is not you and we'll start with most people's starting point in the work field: The Employee.

Business Ownership Mindset

3. **<u>Employee</u>**

When we enter the money world, most often we enter it as an employee. The employee role works great for a few things. For starters it's a great stomping ground for getting your feet wet in the monetary world. It brings in money, which is awesome. It trains you how to start and complete tasks. It may teach you how to set up projects, start them and finish them. It teaches some social skills. There are numerous benefits, obviously, to going out and getting a job.

However, instead of getting excited about the opportunity to learn new skills, take on responsibilities, or find out what they're made of, most people enter the work force or the money realm from a necessity point of view. Usually, it's fear based. "I need to have money", "I need to get something", "My needs aren't being met that way, and I need to have them met this way." It tends to be very fear based and it also tends to be very "school based." In school we're taught: "Sit down, stay quiet, behave like everyone else, don't put your head up, don't look different or act different than anybody else and you'll get along just fine." And those same rules of decorum follow through into the employee world: "Keep your head down, learn everything you can about this 'thing', and be able to regurgitate it when I ask you to, and regurgitate it the way I want you to" I, being the boss. You'll have many different bosses over the years and they'll have many different opinions, just like you had many different teachers and they had many different opinions. But, the stereotype, if you will, is almost exactly the same.

Fortunately for most people, school is the ultimate training ground for the employee position. I say fortunately, because the majority of North American's will become employees and stay that way for the entirety of their working careers. Statistics generally show that between 50 – 70% of the population is employed; however that statistic generally doesn't include government employees or the military, both of which also

Business Ownership Mindset

have employee mentalities.

When it comes to school, "Sit down, face the front, do what I ask you do, and let me know when you're done", is the most common message that a pupil gets. After that it's, "Listen closely, memorize what I say and be able to regurgitate it back to me when I ask for it." Now you might be thinking that those messages don't translate to the workforce, but I assure you that the only reason you would be thinking that is because you never had a corporate office job.

The success or failure of most employees is completely dependent on their ability to sit down, focus on the task that's been given to them and their ability to report their completion to their superior. The only difference is that they usually only have one person to report to, not a multitude of teachers… I mean… managers. ;)

Even in the how-to be a good employee books, they read like a school syllabus:

- Act Professionally; (Behave like everyone else behaves)
- Learn to take criticism; (Accept that you did it wrong and don't talk back)
- Learn what your manager expects of you and deliver; (Your manager is always right)
- Create a positive workspace; (Don't complain or rock the boat)
- Train in upward mobile skill sets; (Know what your superiors expect of you and live up to it)
    - Maintain a clean performance record; (Don't rock the boat, and don't piss anyone off)
    - Be on time; (We are your number one priority, ALWAYS)
    - Ask supervisors what their expectations are; (Don't think for yourself, do what we say)
    - Don't complain;
    - Be quiet at work;

Business Ownership Mindset

- Always be productive;
- The more you do, the more impressed your boss will be;
- Don't spend your time on personal issues;
- Company policies come first;
- Be appreciative of your boss, say thank you;

At first blush this list actually looks great. Be positive, be loyal to the company, and seek advancement. All of that is great, and it will lead to success in the corporate world.

I'm not saying there is anything wrong with this list, but the message is the same as it is in school, and those messages will spell disaster for you in other career positions especially entrepreneurialism, because the mindset for each of those points is very different than the message they're conveying.

Unions, for instance, thrive on everyone being the same. There's an element of upward mobility, but for the most part, length of employment constitutes seniority. In other words, the longer you can keep your head down and not be noticed the more you get promoted and the higher your pay. I'm not saying it's right or wrong. I am saying that unions have a special sort of mindset unto themselves, and if you want to succeed in a union, this is not the book for you. Let's just say that a union mindset is completely outside my wheelhouse.

So what am I saying? I'm saying that the group or mass mentality that allows someone to succeed in school is the same mindset that you need in corporate life in order to succeed;

- Look the same as the people around you.
- Dress like them, walk like them and talk like them.
- Use the same vocabulary and annunciate like they do.
- Fit in with those around you.

Business Ownership Mindset

Learn to take criticism, because there will be criticism and lots of it depending on where you work. Criticism and being reprimanded is part of the culture that got adopted from school and old business. You'll be more successful in that environment accepting it and working with it than to rebel against it. Your manager will likely have been promoted due to excellent skills as a technician of specific tasks and will likely have no skill in management, therefore when they want something done, they won't know how to ask or set you up for success and if it's not done their way, they certainly won't know how to ask for it done the way they want it done, short of knowing what they don't want.

I ask people what their goals are all day, and 90% of the people who are new to me, will tell me what they don't want. Whether it's about their job, their health, their dream spouse, it's all about what they don't want. And, this translates into work. When they're asked what they want, they willingly articulate exactly what they don't want. And, when it is a manager responding it comes across as criticism. This may not be the case in every job, but it's certainly more common than not.

I know, it sounds like I'm not a fan of the employee/ management career path. That's not completely true. I'm not a fan of general lack of training and understanding required to promote people from employee/technician to management, and the neglect and occasionally abuse that comes with it. Having said that, no system is perfect and I've seen plenty of entrepreneurs/business owners who also lacked communication skills and spoke their fair share of criticism. Actually some of them were beyond abusive.

What is important is to understand that in an employee position, not only do you have to gain mental toughness and allow criticism to bounce off of you, you also have to be able to take that criticism and act in accordance with what the manager wants. So, if they say your report wasn't written clearly, you have to figure out what clearly means to them and deliver it to them in that fashion the next time you write a report. In

Business Ownership Mindset

the other career positions, that isn't the case. We'll get into that later.

Learn what your manager expects of you and deliver. It's just like school; learn what your teacher expects of you and deliver it. You have to have the mindset that the teacher is always right and it's your job to adjust to their way of thinking. And, if next month you have a different teacher/manager, you adapt again, to their different way of thinking.

The employee mentality is limited in that the employee is hired to do a task for a pre-negotiated wage and they will only do what is pre-negotiated and the company will only pay what is pre-negotiated. Nothing moves beyond that until another negotiation is completed.

One of the reasons that the employee position is so attractive to many people is that an employee position offers a sense of security that the company will be around and they'll be able to pay a check every two weeks. Some people are so dependent on that thought that they will ensure that their skills and attributes are transferable only to large corporate structures with the promise of longevity so to ensure that they will have this perceived security for the rest of their lives regardless of their natural aptitude and desires.

In short, the company is always right and it is the locus of control. No one is independent of it. That rule applies to everyone from the front end staff to the back end senior staff. If you want to succeed as an employee, know that company rules come first, you do what you're told, you acquire more information to build on the information you had yesterday and you sit down, face the front, do what I ask you do, and let me know when you're done.

Business Ownership Mindset

4. <u>**Sales**</u>

Ah sales. This is most people's stepping-stone to taking control of their day.

Most often the people who outgrow the employee realm want to have a little more independence. They want to have a little bit of autonomy. They will go out into sales knowing that they can start to count on themselves and they can have a little more freedom in their time. They can have a little more freedom in the amount of money they can make, too. They can start to expand beyond the limitations of just what has been given to them.

They may decide that they don't like someone else telling them what to do all day, or they see the freedom in being able to make their own hours, set their own appointments, talk to other people all day and more often than not they see the allure of being able to control their income beyond just hours for a wage. I say more often than not, as the majority of people who go into sales are looking to increase their income. In order to stay in sales people need to be able to shed their security blanket of having a regular check and move their internal security compass to point at themselves and their skills to be able to bring in the money. I love sales because it's like the entrepreneurs playground for learning how to be self-reliant. Don't get me wrong it's not that I see it as fools play. It's not. In fact it's far from it. Most people see sales skills as communication skills or outward social skills; skills that involve an outward ability that they need to acquire. I agree there are some social skills that need to be acquired, but for the most part, if someone focused solely on the inner game of sales, they would succeed much faster than the individual who focuses on the outward sales skills, unless they already have the inner game nailed and they just realized that sales is where they wanted to be in order to succeed.

Business Ownership Mindset

You see, the successful mindset of sales involves being able to separate who you are from what you do. You need to know that who you are, is awesome, solid and unwavering. If you know a variety of sales people, you know that their personalities can be completely different, one from another. One person can be high energy, totally out there, outgoing, super social, extravert, dynamic, mover and shaker and another one at the same company, just as successful can be introverted, demure, quiet, and soft spoken. Being successful in sales does not require that one has an over the top personality, contrary to popular belief. What it does require is a sound belief in one's self, regardless of how that self comes across. We'll be discussing how to succeed at sales more in another chapter, but right now I want to make it clear that there is definitely a different mindset to sales than there is as an employee. The line may get blurred if the sales position is a paid position but from the outside looking in, it becomes very clear that the spectrum of the sales mindset begins at a fully-paid customer service or inside sales position and fans out from there. It fans out through base- plus-commission, commission with quotas and bonuses, to 100% commission with no holds. The predominant mental filter that fades away as you progress through that spectrum is the security and dependence on the company to provide regular finances, systems, guidance and requirements. This is where we see evidence of the law of dichotomy, which states that there is a good and bad to everything, there's and in and an out, an up and a down, every coin has two sides. In the sales realm the sales person really begins to understand that the security that the employee holds onto is also tying them down. The systems which give them structure also limit their creativity and impulse. And, the financial stability they get from a company is limited to the number of hours in a day.

In sales the individual's locus of control, or the source of their strength, is shifting from the company to themselves. This shift doesn't fully complete until one reaches the Business Ownership Mindset, because as a sales representative the individual is still representing the

Business Ownership Mindset

company. In their mind it's still the company that has the reputation, quality products, the service team and all that comes with it. If they're disgruntled with the company's reputation, products and personnel, they can still blame the company; which, all in all, means that the strength still comes from the company, not the individual.

Business Ownership Mindset

5. <u>Management</u>

Management can look like a tough one to nail down a specific mindset for because you can arrive there from so many angles. Some people come into it after getting a business degree, some people prove to be the best technician or sales person and get promoted, some people fail as technician or sales person and get promoted, and others just land there due to who they know in the company. As you can guess I'm going to say after having read the last section, there are pros and cons to all of these methods of attainment. But, oddly enough, none of them are necessarily better than the others in preparing someone to be in a management mindset at the point of entry. After getting a business degree, the individual potentially has a ton of knowledge on communication, leadership, business acumen, and so on. But, rarely do they have any experience managing a team of people! They have what we refer to as having knowledge of how to do it, but no experience doing it. And knowledge and experience are two very different animals!

The person who fails as a technician and gets promoted is ironically, likely the best way to arrive in a management position, if they were promoted for the right reason. If the individual was hired because they had an aptitude for gathering the troops, motivating others, creating a team atmosphere and getting the resources together that the team needed to succeed, then they will make an excellent manager, other than they may lack some business knowledge that they need to really succeed. More often than not, that's pretty easy to come by, but it will take time and effort. These individuals are often not the top performers as technicians because they lack the ability to focus on the task at hand and get it done. They often are more sociable and see the big picture and get bored with details. Those could be qualified as personality traits, but when it comes to mindset, they've bypassed mastering detail orientation and if you'd like you could say that they haven't mastered the employee

Business Ownership Mindset

mindset. In a corporate setting, this could come back to bite them as they will still need certain employee mindset components to get them out of middle management and into upper management. After all, in a corporate environment, the employee mentality runs all the way through the corporation.

There are also the ones who get promoted for other reasons than competency in management. Their competency might be in politics and they're simply climbing the corporate ladder. They might excel at being lazy and creating systems to do the least amount of work (that one has obvious pros and cons). These types of managers tend to have the social realm of management mindset down, but lack the technical competence or even the team building competence. They may well still be in it for themselves. Their ability to gain the management mindset will be vital to them, or their careers can lead to one short and frightening stint after another.

The individual who succeeded at being the best technician or sales person who gets promoted has important experiential knowledge that they can share as a manager with their team for sure! However, the management mentality is totally different than the master technician mindset, in that the master technician is very self-focused. They have to be. In order to master sales and be a rock star, they have to depend on themselves, know that at the end of the day they're the only one they can count on to get the job done and a multitude of other self-focused beliefs. In order to transition into management, they are going to have to learn how to share their knowledge, be patient with others, teach others, and at the end of the day depend on someone else to get the job done. This group as a whole tend to make the worst managers because they give their teams too much room and not enough direction. They will benefit from training and attention to let go of their technician mindset and move into a management mindset.

Lastly we have the fortunate, or unfortunate, ones who get put

Business Ownership Mindset

into management because of who they know. This may seem like a godsend from the outside, but it can be hell on the inside. Depending on the individual's personality and the support they have going into this role, they may succeed nicely or fall flat on their face. They need to learn everything; the business, the technical details, the social atmosphere, how to lead a team and how to follow orders. Their best chance for success is having a mindset of loving trial by fire, of loving steep growth curves, of feeling that the more extreme the challenge the better the game. The good news is that, if they survive and succeed at that, their climb up the ladder is shorter and sweeter because they're now thinking that quick rise is the norm and that's the way it always should be. They, typically, are your "A-Type" personalities.

Business Ownership Mindset

6. **<u>Entrepreneur</u>**

Entrepreneurs tend to be your "wildcats" of society. Often they felt like they didn't fit in at school or at work or even in social settings. Regardless of whether they are introverts or extroverts, whether they felt superior, inferior or just outside of the group, they tend to see themselves as "not like the rest of them". And, coincidentally, their peers or parents often saw them in the same way. They'll say things like, "Tommy was always a pro on the field, he got great marks, but he didn't have any real friends." Or "Sally was always off doing her own thing and we never knew what the next thing would be." It's not like they're socially inept or unsuccessful. In fact most times, it is the opposite; they're very successful in certain realms. But, when it comes down to it, they'd rather take the bulls by the horn and get things done on their own terms in their own way and they don't want anyone else slowing them down. Some people are born this way, some people are conditioned and brought up this way, and some people grow into it, or just wake up one day and think, "There's got to be a better way!"

The difference between sales and an entrepreneur is that the entrepreneur isn't selling a widget, they're selling themselves. They're not selling someone else's idea. They're selling their own. It is WAY easier to sell somebody else or their ideas than it is to sell yourself.

Some entrepreneurs will say, "I'm not selling myself. I'm selling my widget. It's my widget, so that's ok." But to really get into the entrepreneurial mindset and become truly successful you need to be able to sell yourself.

I'll give you an example of a friend of mine whom I've known since elementary school. Her mother was a dog groomer and handler and she owned a few dog grooming salons in town. Her father was an engineer and he ran his own company, too. Since the early age of five she

Business Ownership Mindset

was groomed (pun intended), to be a world-class dog handler and groomer. Now if you're not familiar with that world, don't feel left out, most people aren't. Every dog handler knows that there is a certain aspect to winning a show that is about the dog, as everyone might suspect. But, what they also know, especially the good ones, is that there is a high element of handler confidence and personality that is required to win. It's as if the dog and handler are a team. The handler has to know who they are and what they bring to the ring in order for the dog to win a ribbon. No matter how world-class the dog is, the dog cannot win without an equally confident handler. Now, what does this have to do with being an entrepreneur, you ask? Well my friend, as you might suspect, has an extreme level of personality and confidence considering she's been primed for it almost her entire life. At school she was extremely popular and a lot of fun to be around. She was never, what you might describe as, a loner, but she did always feel different from the crowd and she was. The crowd followed her. Everywhere.

    The reason I want to create an image for you is that I want you to see what I really mean by this feeling of being different. You may say that everyone feels different from the crowd and no one really feels "normal," but that's not true. There are many people who love to be a part of the crowd and to fit in. And that's great! I simply believe that the more you can understand this feeling, the easier it is to understand the inner push that drives someone to start their own business and why they do it. Why you might even do it. And, I'd like you to realize that this feeling, like all others, can change. Even though someone might love being part of a group for most of their lives, that feeling may change later in life. There are no steadfast rules to it, but there are indicators. Where these indicators become important is when someone is banging their head against the proverbial wall and not succeeding the way they want to, and when they have this crazy idea or notion that they should go it on their own. That idea...well...it just might not be that crazy after all.

Business Ownership Mindset

7. <u>Business Ownership Mindset</u>

The brutal truth of reality is that even though the essence of who we are as human beings is to grow mentally, emotionally and experientially as much as we possibly can in our short little lifetimes, not everyone feeds into that essence. Some get cut down in their prime and refuse to get up and grow, again. Some get complacent and think that what they see is what they get and that's all there is to life. And others have their reasons too. But every once in a while there is an individual who simply isn't satisfied with status quo and they want more. They want to experience life to its fullest, they want to test their limits and see what they're made of, and they have this inner drive and inspiration to create, produce, and experience more. That is the individual who takes on the Business Ownership Mindset.

Business Ownership Mindset essentially is having a vision of your company that far surpasses you and what you can do as an individual. It's what you can create with a team of people to impact the world in a far greater way than you can do on your own. It's building a well-oiled machine that ideally could run on its own and you wouldn't even have to step foot in it again and you'd get paid for life and possibly beyond that. In order to build something of that magnitude you have to be willing to see things in a certain way, think in a certain way, act in a certain way. That way requires that you use all of the resources you have mentally, emotionally and physically. It requires that you use those personal resources to fully express yourself so that people will follow you, so that they will take on your vision and call it their own. It requires that you trust the people around you to take on your vision and possibly expand on it, growing it more than you would have. And, understand that not only is that ok, it's ideal.

Now, obviously, not everyone is going to come up with a recipe in their mom and pop shop for a cola and turn it into the Coca-Cola

Business Ownership Mindset

behemoth that exists today. And, not everyone is going to tinker in their garage with some wires and cables to build a computing box that turns into the Apple Computers of today. But, there will be thousands if not millions of people who step out of the solopreneur realm and embrace the Business Ownership Mindset either consciously or subconsciously to breathe life into their dream and become more than just self-expressive, but to become something greater than the sum of its parts.

The good news is that there are skills that you can develop consciously to maximize your competence and efficiency. And, the great news is that you already have within you what it takes to pull this off. You just have to draw it out of yourself.

Business Ownership Mindset

8. In Conclusion

In the expansion of mindsets from our earliest involvement of the consumer phase all the way to The Business Ownership Mindset we will constantly be evolving to some extent whether we allow for it or not. As I said at the beginning, some people learn how to self-actualize in the consumer state and never have to leave it. They understand the value they bring to the table; they sell themselves, their knowledge or their skills without ever having to get involved in commerce.

Learning and seeing how we are constantly selling ourselves is paramount. Whether it's to our mothers for the Sunday treat, during a job interview, in a boardroom presentation, in a speech to our volunteer supporters or to our staff; it is all selling ourselves. It's simply to what flavour are you selling yourself? It's the depth, breadth and color with which we do that which will change our inner strength, and hence our outer influence.

Understand that there are some people who evolve in the corporate world, understanding how to sell themselves and make it to the top of the corporate ladder without rocking the boat too much, or putting their head up too high.

The ideal to me, as weird as this may sound, is to stay in consumerism. We wouldn't have a monetary system, we wouldn't need it. We'd be able to consciously bypass it. I say that, because it unto itself is a fear based system. It relies on the idea that I won't get back my value, that I need to have some sort of way of assessing what that value is and how I know that something is mine, and that I own it and then I have to hold on to it somehow some way, but, if we could bypass that somehow and just know that we have our wealth, we have our "whatever we value in society" and that whatever we bring to society, will be brought back to us. But, for now we have to depend on the architecture that exists now.

Business Ownership Mindset

Don't misunderstand me I don't think living a life of poverty is healthy. In fact, it's the exact opposite. I agree with George Bernard Shaw when he said that it's a sin to be poor. Not accepting the value in return for the value you bring to the table is equally dysfunctional to "needing" money. Needing, in the fear based thought that money is everything and everything else is nothing.

On the functional healthy side of consumerism we have the Dalai Lama, or Mother Theresa, who owned nothing but have and had access to great wealth. And they have that access mostly because they are self-actualized and know how to sell themselves. They know who they are, they know what their value is and they no longer have resistance to value or money or to those concepts.

It's not that they were born a certain way. It's that they opened up to that stream of consciousness and the opportunities open up for them. You have to have that ideal which says, it's not important for me to hoard money, it's not important for me to shy away from worldly duties, it's just important for me to be me, who I am.

If you want the fastest easiest way to self-actualization by allowing yourself to stand up, rock the boat, and put a whole lot of personality into what you do while living in a monetary system, then you'll want to study the entrepreneurial mindset, and then master The Business Ownership Mindset.

Business Ownership Mindset

Chapter 2
Business as a form of Self-Expression

When the entrepreneur learns to "fly" they set up their business in such a way that ideally they can utilize their talents and traits to the best of their ability to express themselves fully. It just makes sense that someone who is an engineer will likely start up an engineering firm, or at least be in a company full of engineers, caters to engineers, or allows the individual to pursue intellectual pursuits of that calibre. From the outside looking in, it seems pretty evident that someone of that capacity would be most content, if not happiest, in such an environment. But what happens when we get convinced that veering off course would be more profitable, or have more promise of opportunity? If an individual isn't true to themselves, or know what they truly want, it's easy to get taken off track and create a state of misery for ourselves.

On the other end of the spectrum, there are engineers who only became engineers because it was the thing to do. Maybe their marks were high in math, or their parents nudged them in that direction, but in their heart they really wanted to pursue something else. These individuals may find themselves in a business that they too are miserable in. And, they start to ask themselves, "How did I get myself into this mess???" or "There's got to be a better way, isn't there?"

Businesses tend to be the most successful when the soon to be business owner takes an inventory of who they are, what they like, and what they want to deliver. Sadly, most people will look around at other companies and assess which of those they like the best. In the world of true self-expression it works much better when someone says, "I want to do this", regardless of whether or not "this" exists yet or not. It's a matter of being able to listen to your heart and asking yourself, "If I could do it

Business Ownership Mindset

any way I wanted to, what would I do?" It's in that creative passion that ideas flow and true success happens.

The people who take inventory of the business ideas available to them are starting off at a disadvantage in that the existing molds may not have robustness available to them to keep the entrepreneur engaged and passionate about moving forward. And, when it comes down to it, it's up to the entrepreneur to be passionate in order to keep the business moving forward.

So here are some questions you might want to ask yourself:

Where's your sweet spot to get you in the zone?

Where is your passion?

Where are your fields of competence?

What would you love to get paid to do?

How do you start delegating the rest?

If you could delegate all the rest of the things you feel you have to do in a day, what could that ideally look like?

When would you like to have that done by "realistically"?

Ya, ya, everyone wants it done yesterday, but when could you actually have it done by?

Business Ownership Mindset

1. <u>The type of business we choose</u>

There is a myriad of business styles to choose from, whether they are retail, wholesale, corporate, network marketing, one on one consulting, masterminds, retreats, writing, government, unionized, franchised, internet based, and the list goes on. There are singular models and there are combination models. And, in case it's not obvious, there are more to yet be invented. Certain models will appeal more to one individual than another and the reason, I believe, it's important to define this for yourself is that some models won't appeal long term to certain personality types. For example in the coaching industry I cannot tell you how many people I come across who are sociable, outgoing who want to change the world, who love being in groups and love commanding attention. If they set up their business to only do one on one coaching, even if it is live and face to face, they're going to be miserable long term because they won't have the degree of social interaction that they need to feel self-actualized. Likewise, there are the introverted, intellectual types who start corporate offices where everyone reports to them. It's going to be a hard run to keep that business up and running, because it hasn't taken into account the high degree of social interaction that is required in a corporate setting.

    Ultimately if an entrepreneur wants to be as successful as they can be, they have much higher odds of success starting with a business model that suites their personality and traits than it does to look for the model with the highest success rate and hope that they can take it to those heights.

    When we are not conscious of the choices we make and we simply go by habit into our business, our personal issues will find a way to surface, present themselves, and force us to deal with them. As was once said, "Everywhere we go, there we are." In this case I mean that whether in your personal life or your business life, you will make decisions to

Business Ownership Mindset

create circumstances to prove you right, and if you have the belief that you never get any time to yourself, you'll prove that true in your business. If you have beliefs that say you're lonely, you'll prove that true in your business.

If, on the other hand, you go into business knowing who you are and what you want, you'll build time in for yourself, or you'll build in social aspects, whatever you require.

Business Ownership Mindset

2. The way we deal with others

Most people think they can separate their personal life from their business life and how they deal with one aspect is separate from the other. This makes me laugh.

The issue is that no matter where I go, there I am. How you deal with people is simply how you correspond with them. Even if you think, "This is a professional relationship and that is a personal relationship."

The idioms are still going to shine through. Whether it's the snickers, or the sarcasm, or the sweetness, or the consideration. Whatever 'it' is will still come through, because that's just you. In understanding this, we will also set up our corporations this way.

As I mentioned in the last section, the way in which we ideally interact with people really should be taken into consideration when we start a company. There are so many personality typing companies out there and they are so accessible that it doesn't make sense to me to start a business without knowing "who you are" first. And, no I don't mean your name and address. I mean qualities such as introverted or extroverted. And now that I've said this is easy and accessible, I'll shake the table a bit.

According to the most available definitions out there introverted and extroverted refer to whether or not someone is outgoing or reflective, if they are the centre of attention or hidden in the shadows. I have a different opinion of these words and I think it's important to differentiate here, not only for clarification of the terms, but more importantly so that you can get a better understanding of who you are. In my experience we need to separate a few personality traits from the introverted/extroverted spectrum.

There are people who enjoy being in the company of others and it gives them energy when they're down. There are at the other end people

Business Ownership Mindset

who tolerate being in the company of others and it drains them of their energy. And there are all the ones in between who know that there can be too much of a good thing, and they appreciate both being around people and their solitude. The reason you want to know where you fall in this spectrum is because there are business models that appeal to all three types. You want to set up your company so that it can facilitate and harness your drive and energy. If you're drained being around people, then you may want to reconsider starting up a network marketing company. If you need to have other people around you to get energized and motivated, you may want to reconsider starting a home based consulting business. I'm not saying there aren't work-a-rounds, but if you can start up your company within the consideration of your social styles, you'll likely be more successful.

The second aspect of the introverted/extroverted scale is the way people tackle problem solving. When someone needs to talk about the aspects of a problem to vocalize them (whether anyone else is listening/present/ or otherwise) we refer to them as being extroverted. However this same person may socially be introverted. And this is where the confusion comes from. So, I separate Social Introverted/Extroverted from Problem Solving Introverted/Extroverted. In my experience, they have nothing to do with each other.

The individual who needs to think and reflect on the information first before they come to a conclusion and verbalize their thoughts will be in a different communication style than their problem solving counterpart. They tend to succeed in different positions within a company but it has not been my experience that one will succeed in a different business model over the other. Both can be very intellectual and analytical, and both styles can be very sociable and humanitarian. The important part here is if you know that you are sociable and you like to have sounding boards around you to problem solve, you probably want to create a business, or adjust your current business to accommodate having

Business Ownership Mindset

other people around you on a frequent basis. If on the other hand you are private and you need to have time in silence to consider your issues of the day, you'll want to make sure that your business model accommodates that style.

Ideally you want to create a business that reflects your style. (Or modify your current business to reflect your style.) Because if it doesn't reflect that, if we're really introverted and we hate being around people and we start a networking company where we have to be around people all the time, or we open a bar where we have to be there all the time and we have to be "on" all the time we're going to drive ourselves insane. How we take this into consideration is by asking yourself, "How do I communicate? How do I like to communicate? Is this business that I'm in appropriate for my style? What would be the most appropriate for my style so that I'm not feeling like a complete misfit all the time?"

It would be like me finding a corporate job now and thinking, "Oh this is so not appropriate." Right? You know it, and I know it. I'm going to talk to people the way that I talk to people both in my personal life and in my professional life and I'm going to think that they get it, or that they get me and they're not going to get it. And that, would only get me into trouble. It's not to say I can't do contract work within a corporation, though. In that role people will expect me to communicate different and act different than an employee. Therefore, with the same communication style, I can be extremely effective as a consultant or outsourced trainer whereas I would flop as an employee.

Now we can move this into a generalization of personality types and natural skills and how those qualities translate into being effective in a role and it becomes obvious how we become more effective when our natural talents and passions are combined and utilized to our advantage.

A question to ask yourself if you are in corporate is how many of your staff feel like they have split personality where they feel they can be

Business Ownership Mindset

one way at home and they have to be another way at work? And, how much stress does that put on the individual because they aren't being their authentic self? What does that stress do to them, and to their performance, and to the quality of the company's results? And better yet, how much better would they feel in an authentic roll? How much would their performance increase and how much would the quality of their work improve?

That is one of the reasons that companies have such low output. What if they hired people that actually wanted to be in those positions, and excelled in those positions naturally?

All too often people get jobs because they think, "This is the only skill set I have." Or "How much can I get paid to do it?" Or "This is the way I have to go because this is the way my parents want me to go."

So many people end up in an occupation that they may be really good at but they hate, but they would be much better off at an occupation that they really like but they aren't that good at.

As so eloquently put in his book "Now Discover Your Strength", Marcus Buckingham essentially says that successful companies with successful leadership asked, "What are some of the strengths that you leveraged?" and they discovered that when a company can identify the strength of their people and utilize those strengths that are coupled with passion that they build their company from the individual up. And, they defined those strengths not only as what they're good at, but what they have a talent for, knowledge about and skills with.

It's been said that there are skills that we have that we have mastered, but we're not passionate about and pursuing these skills will lead us to a life of misery. I believe this is because there is no room to stretch and grow in that circumstance; that pursuing the skills where we have a talent and an interest even though we may not have mastered them yet, gives us room to grow and lead a fulfilled life.

Business Ownership Mindset

I think it's important to understand the difference between a talent, a skill and a personality trait. What Marcus would call a talent; I might call a personality trait. That would be something that comes so naturally to you that you don't even know you're good at it; something such as empathy, or decisiveness. These are aspects that will transfer in communication style from personal to business relationships whether we notice them or not. Talent, to me, is a skill that we pick up quickly and seemingly effortlessly and a skill, in this case, is an action or behaviour that can be learned.

Bringing the conversation back to specifically our means of communication; our natural forms of communication will come through in all of our relationships. When we build a company, it's important to know our individual style because it, and it will manifest itself into our company, and you want to make sure that it builds and makes your company.

Business Ownership Mindset

3. <u>The value we feel we bring to the table.</u>

Each and every person on this planet has numerous skills that are both innate, and developed. The whole reason we go into business in the first place is because we know that internally we have something that's bigger than ourselves that just needs to be expressed. And, it can't be expressed in a 'job' because the job is too confining and too dependent on somebody else, and we just need to break free and go, "BAM! Here I am!"

It doesn't matter what it is. It could be going out and buying pens, and selling pens! But there's something in there that says, "I'm the best at selling pens", or "I see a way that it can be done better", or "I have a vision that pens are going to be everywhere, and I have a vision that pens need to be everywhere!" Awesome! Then that's you and your business!

When it comes to running a company, each and every one of our passionate skills can be nourished, developed and monetized. There isn't a person out there who doesn't have a skill that can't be monetized; all it requires is some creativity, determination and the right support. If you don't believe me, look around. There are companies who hire autistic people for their fantastic ability to do everything from data entry to accounting. There are people working at hospitals to hug and hold babies during their long term stays. There are people who get paid to pick up recycling in offices and drop it off, all the while being supervised themselves and driven around because they are incapable of driving and holding themselves accountable. If people can figure out what their abilities are, what things come easily to them or what they love to do and get better at, then they can find a way to monetize it.

Understand that no matter where you are at right now, if you can read this book that you have hireable skills, and if you have hireable skills then you can figure out a way to start a company from those skills. Now you may be in a position where you already run a company but you want

Business Ownership Mindset

to change direction or take it up a notch, in that case, you have to believe that if they can do it, you can do it! If someone with little to seemingly no skill can start a company and make a go of it, then you can too! It simply requires some brain storming!

Now this doesn't mean that just because we have one skill that we will run a company from it, but it doesn't mean that we won't either. All businesses require some help and support and when you have a Business Ownership Mindset, you know that you'll want people around you. It'll be part of the plan! So you definitely want to identify what skills you don't have that you think would be vital to the company. Some of these people might be volunteers, they may work part time, full time, or out sourced. They may be a temporary solution or permanent. They might be what you can afford now or they may even be the best in the industry. Regardless of what you require, there is someone out there who has the skills and experience that you require and they want to share those skills with you! Remember, everyone has a value that they bring to the table. If you can think of it, someone has that skill.

This brings us to why it's important to us to express our qualities. Everyone has the desire to master skills and be considered good at them. Sometimes, I'll grant you, good is good enough for some people, but we all have that desire. Whether we bring information to the table, action, connection or organization we all have skills to bring to the table and we like having a feeling of accomplishment and fulfilment regardless of how we get it. When we aren't challenging ourselves, accomplishing things, or being all we can be in a moment we feel like there's something more to life, but we don't necessarily know what it is. We feel disappointed. When we are challenging ourselves and we are accomplishing things and we're being all that we can be we are in flow; we are being expressive we're giving all that we have and it feels great.

When successful people feel shallow and unfulfilled it isn't because they need to have more things, or accomplish more tasks, it is

Business Ownership Mindset

that they need to identify what they really want in their hearts to express and they need to figure out a way to challenge themselves to do it. That might mean that they need to say something to someone, it might mean that they need to shift their life direction or it could be an infinite number of things in between there. But in the end, they need to be the one to identify that. They need to ask themselves seriously and with heart, "What do I need to do to feel challenged, to feel like I'm accomplishing something and to be all that I can be?"

And know that what you need to do or feel does not come from someone else. If you say something like, "I just need to be acknowledged for my work." Then, I'm sorry but that's wrong. You don't need to be acknowledged by someone else. You need to figure out internally, whatever it is that you need to figure out in order to get that feeling of challenge, accomplishment, or satisfaction internally. As Wayne Dyer said many times, "If you're waiting for everyone else to change before you can be happy, you're going to be miserable every day of your life."

The feelings that accompany fulfillment come from internal sources that you need to find, discover, or uncover from within yourself. It may take meditation, pondering or focused action to find it, but I assure you; it's inside of you, not outside

To bring it back to the discussion in the previous chapter, it could be a matter of looking at what talents you have naturally, AND identifying the passions you have even if it's in a seemingly polar opposite field.

I've worked with a lawyer that wanted to be a truck driver, and he became a far happier more fulfilled truck driver than he ever was as a lawyer. I've worked with executives that wanted to be consultants, accountants that wanted to be healers, athletes that wanted to run their own business and nurses who wanted to be artists. They all had the same modus operandi, "I have to do this because it pays more. I don't want to be broke." And, wildly enough, they are all making more money now in

Business Ownership Mindset

their new career than they were in their previous one. And, maybe it was because they worked with me, maybe it was because they had a coach, maybe it was because they allowed themselves to follow their passion, or maybe it was all of the above. All I know, is that this is just a few examples, I have a ton more! And they all thought that they were bringing their top skills to the table until they realized that they needed to bring their passion with them.

The journey is being able to overcome the fear of doing something that we're not necessarily good at. If we can follow the love of doing something we break through all the barriers.

Do you want to know what your talents are and where your passion lies? A simple way to do this is to take stock of your behaviours in a day and notice, those activities that you get done and then you look at the clock and exclaim, "Wow! It's been 6 hours already!?!?" that's your passion. But, when you're looking at the clock and thinking, "Am I done yet?... Am I done yet?...How about now?" You may be good at that thing, but it's not your passion. When you're doing stuff, to avoid doing the thing, you know you can do but you don't want to. That may not be your passion.

Now I'm going to throw a caveat in the mix. Some people will avoid doing something because they're afraid of the outcome. This is especially obvious in sales. So many people will hate prospecting and making calls because they don't like the rejection or the monotony of making calls. That does not mean that they can't be passionate about sales. What it means is that they have some fear to overcome in order to practice and play out their passion. You may need help to overcome the fear, and that is certainly possible! We do it every day in our practice. And, once you see it as a game or an opportunity to connect with people, and you let go of 'their stuff' then you can unleash your passion even greater, in this case, around sales.

Business Ownership Mindset

However, if you find yourself lost in sales calls loving every minute of it, then you have found your passion and it will be easy for you to see what you bring to the business table.

From a corporate position, it can't be that hard to see that your company will be that much more productive when you have someone who loves what they do running a position with enthusiasm, versus having someone twiddling their fingers trying to get to the end of the day. You want people who are enthusiastic and effective.

Business Ownership Mindset

4. The "problem" we have that's to be solved.

Innately not only do we have talents that need to be expressed, we also have a problem that needs to be solved, but we don't know how to solve it. And, we won't know how to solve it until we do 'this thing.'

It's the proverbial psychologist who has more issues than everyone else, so he opens an office as a psychologist not so much to solve everyone else's issues, although he does have a passion to help other people, he has this issue that he needs to figure out and it's through helping others that somebody comes in the office and says, "Hey I have this problem," and through his willingness to solve their problem that he goes, "Oh I get it!" and figures out his own issue.

Even if we go back to the last conversation about the pen company's business owner, even though he loves doing it, there's something that he's created a problem for himself that he needs to solve. It might be something such as distribution and he feels like he's being spread too thin and he has to have a big company that is spread too thin in order solve or resolve that problem.

It's not so much that the problems we get into in our company are bad or that the problems that we have are bad and that they're not allowed to be expressed, but that the reason we've gone into business for ourselves is to crack that egg.

There are a whole multitude of things that are going on when a person starts their company that they don't really get. They may think that they're just frustrated with corporate world and they simply want to go out and start their own company. And I think, "Well that's cute." ☺

It is a most interesting concept that happens with people. It happens in their daily lives and it most certainly happens in their careers and there is no exception to the businesses they open. We will build into our company our own problems, life queries, or dysfunctions. Most

Business Ownership Mindset

owners of companies who discover a problem within their company will want to hire someone to solve their employee's problems, but what they don't realize is that they themselves have created the problem.

From another perspective, I can tell you what the business owner is like based on how the company runs. I can walk into a company, see how it runs and I have a really good idea of what the president is like. It's not only the culture, it's the branding, and it's the way people interact with each other; it's the culmination of the business. Everything about a business stems from the owner. From yet another perspective, if you talk to marketing companies, sales training companies, business strategists; anyone who deals with a company from the outside who can see a problem in a company, they all know that the problems they see stem from the top. Likewise it might be a fantastic company, and they can see that 'IT' starts from the top. Whoever is in charge of the company, their personality permeates through the entire company.

As a wantopreneur or solopreneur you want to understand that 'who I am' as a person is going to permeate through my company. Essentially, know that the higher up you are in the chain of command, your personality is going to ripple down throughout the company. And, it's not a matter of leadership and authority of decisions; but my issues as an individual are going to manifest throughout my company whether I want them to or not. What I create is a reflection of who I am. If we don't understand where the source of our issues is emanating, then we don't know where to go to solve the problem. If I think that the problem I have is my staff over there having a problem, then I'm going to try to fix my staff over there. But I'm completely overlooking that the problem could be stemming from me. Even if all I did was to ask myself, "How do I feel about the problem that's going on over there?", "What's really going on with me?", "What does that remind me of?", and "Where does that previous answer come from?"

When we as business owners give ourselves permission to ask

Business Ownership Mindset

these questions, we start to get answers like, "Oh my Gawd, my sister's had this nittershit going on and they ALWAYS had this nittershit going on. They would always get into arguments over nittershit; it used to drive me nuts. I have to get over that." And once the owner 'gets over' that(I'll show you how in a later chapter, in case it takes more than just reason to have the epiphany and truly 'get over' it.), then the nittershit with the staff over there quits happening, either on its own or because it is now being dealt with in a different way. Yes, it goes beyond just stepping in and resolving the staff issue over there, and looking at it as "this is my issue" and in order to resolve this issue I have to resolve it in me first. Because if I don't resolve it in me, and I just fire everyone who has the issue, the next group of staff to take their place will likely have the same issue if not more intensely. The good news is that because it's my issue, I can resolve it. I'll say it again. What I create is a reflection of who I am. And, my business is definitely my creation.

We all know that our thoughts lead to our feelings, our feelings lead to our actions and our actions lead to our results, but not everyone knows what their results are, and I'm saying here that they are your everything. If it's happening in your world, it's your results. If it's happening in your business, it's definitely your results. And, again, the great part is that if you take accountability for this process of creation, then you can change your results and resolve the issues that arise in your company; large or small, by changing your thoughts.

At this point, some people will argue, "Well, yes I chose my house, but I didn't choose that it would have sewage problems. I didn't pick that it would be in a flood zone."

And, my answer is, "Does your house have sewage problems? Is it in a flood zone? If the answer is yes, then yes, you did. You know you did, because those are your results. Now, it may not have been a conscious choice, but it had to have been a subconscious choice, because you

Business Ownership Mindset

created it. It is within the realm of your results."

Thoughts aren't just the ideas running around in your head that you ramble on about. Most of those aren't even thoughts. That's just the tape playing over and over again. But, the beliefs that we have, those thoughts, those billions of pieces to the puzzle, create our reality.

It's like the boss who berates his management in meetings who doesn't get called on it by his managers, will likely find himself in the thick of things when management is berating their staff and their staff aren't just disgruntled with their jobs, they aren't just quitting because of it, but they themselves are berating the company and even suing the company for harassment. He has the opportunity to look at the situation and ask himself, "Where do I do that? Where do I get so angry that I bite back at the people who support me?" In that light, if he can recognize that those are his results, then he can bring it back to his thoughts that are creating that result, which in this example happens to be that he actually berates his staff.

Just to hammer the thought home; have you ever had the experience where you've had two teachers for the same class, let's say English class. In that class, in order to get A's, did you write differently for those two teachers? Yes, absolutely you did. Part of it was because they told you what they wanted you to write, and part of it was because you just knew their personality and you knew what they wanted, right? So follow that train of thought with me: What if you had a partner, and you hired an HR person who's in charge of hiring your team and they know that they have one boss, you, that wants certain employees and they have another boss who wants a different set of certain employees. Do you think that they're going to, consciously or otherwise, start hiring differently for their two bosses? Yes. Absolutely.

Let's take it a step further, if you were the boss with more seniority and you have the final say in every decision that goes on in your

Business Ownership Mindset

company, you can't think that that ripple effect isn't going to take place for everyone in your company. It is. They know that you have an expectation of how they are supposed to behave and they respond in kind. In order for them to change the way they react, just like a little kid at home, you the parent have to change the way you act and then they will change the way they act. Now, it might not be immediate, because they might not trust the change at first. They might look at you inquisitively and think, "Really? Is that just for this week? Is it going to last?"

And, when you do it for a couple of months and it lasts...then they will trust you and they will make the changes.

It's just like at home, the older your kids are the longer it's going to take for them to change aptly. The younger your kids are, the faster they're going to change when you change. At work, the less time they've been employed with you the quicker they are to change, and the longer they've been with you the longer it's going to take for them to accept that you have changed and move into the change with you.

Business Ownership Mindset

Chapter 3
Self-Actualization
and the importance of it.

1. <u>Maslow's hierarchy and the flipside of it.</u>

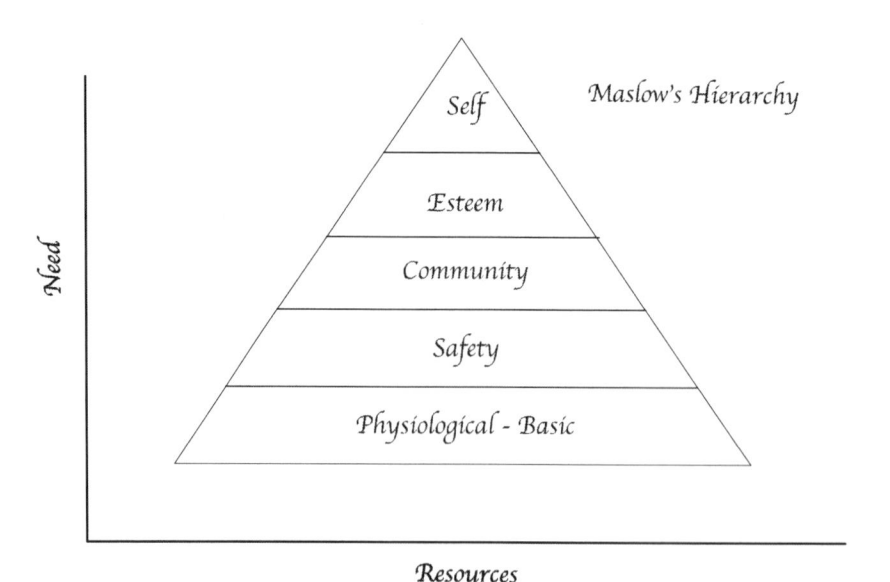

Maslow's Hierarchy

(Pyramid from top to bottom: Self, Esteem, Community, Safety, Physiological - Basic)

Y-axis: *Need*
X-axis: *Resources*

I'm certain you've seen Maslow's hierarchy of needs.

It first came out in his paper on A Theory of Human Motivation. Since then, little has changed; we all seem to agree that the theory is sound. People are motivated to have our physiologically needs met first. Then once those needs are met, we are motivated to be safe. After that we are motivated to belong. After that is in place we are motivated to find love. After that is in place we are motivated to find our self-esteem and lastly we are motivated to self-actualize.

Business Ownership Mindset

As I see it, most people will go through these steps one at time starting with the foundation and moving their way up. Unfortunately, some people will get stuck along the way and not move past the section that they are in. I don't know if it's because they've been conditioned to stay there, or because they forget that there is somewhere else to grow, or if there is another reason. Not that those two reasons are far off of each other. And, Maslow didn't study that either. He studied the successful people of this time, the 1% of the population, to formulate the basis of his theory. What I have done is studied what it takes for people to become self-actualized and I turned Maslow's hierarchy upside down with a time scale on the horizontal axis. The way he has it set up, and the way most people tend to live by it, is that they tend to spend the majority of their time satisfying their basic needs and less and less time on each level as they go up. Once they have everything in place, then they can start to self-actualize. But if we flip it upside down and we spend the majority of our time in self-actualization, and the least amount of our time worrying about our basic needs, then they all get met.

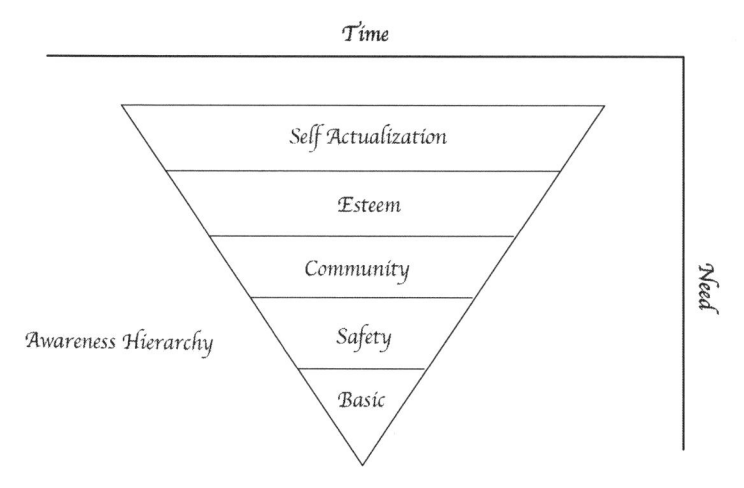

Time

Awareness Hierarchy

- Self Actualization
- Esteem
- Community
- Safety
- Basic

Need

Business Ownership Mindset

So if we can figure out what that thing is that allows us to self-actualize, going back to our example that I'm the world's greatest pen salesperson, great! Go start a company. Go be the world's greatest salesperson. Go figure it out and your basic needs will be met. You'll be building your esteem. You'll be building your community. You'll be building your safety and you'll be building your basic needs.

Now, what I'm talking about is a little more difficult in certain circumstances. Let's go back to the traditional corporate world where it's almost like a war zone. Where you have a competitive and cutthroat environment where bullets are constantly flying at you. How do you not focus on your basic needs? You're always fighting fire and thinking about the future 'later.'

A great friend of mine was in charge of the planning department of a huge utility company and he never got to plan. They were always doing Just-in-Time planning. The fires are so high and come so fast because someone didn't plan properly. When there was a lull in the economy and they should have been taking advantage of it to plan, the future looked bleak so they couldn't plan to build because their budgets were being cut, employees being laid off, so their time was being over maxed, and they had to figure out how to do crisis control. That happens in corporate, and it's happening right now at the time of this book writing. They had 4 to 6 billion dollars in future projects planned, but because the price of oil went down the forecasts showed that they didn't need the project in place anymore.

It's like the city I live in. It's one of the fastest growing cities, but they don't want to spend the money on huge infrastructure of roads for people who aren't here yet. Once the people come, they'll build the roads to accommodate. I'm not going to beat this dead horse because I could write a book on this particular city's backwards planning and how they cost themselves so much by thinking that they're controlling growth. Ok, yes I will. It makes no sense whatsoever to build a 4 lane highway and

Business Ownership Mindset

build a bridge over it that only accommodates two lanes, waiting until the population grows to tear down the bridge and have it then built to accommodate the four lanes beneath it. Ok, I'm done my rant. These are really simple things that people in decision making positions are struggling with.

My point is this; if you spend the majority of your time on basic needs then you will never have the time to self-actualize. Spend more time self-actualizing and the basic needs will work themselves out. I'll cover more on this in another chapter.

Business Ownership Mindset

2. What is Self-Actualization?

Self-Actualization was the word that Maslow used in A Theory of Human Motivation borrowed, as noted in the paper, from Kurt Goldstein to encapsulate "the desire for self-fulfillment, namely the tendency for (one) to become actualized in what he is potentially. This tendency might be phrased as the desire to become more and more what one is, to become everything that one is capable of becoming."

Self-Actualization is a beautiful state that every human being longs to experience. We all have a burning ember of hope within us that we can be happy, that we can experience more of life, that we can do something awesome and amazing. In some people it is so hidden behind the veils of illusion that say, "I'm not good enough", "I can't do this", "Who am I to want more?", "Be satisfied with what you have", "People like me don't get more, ever." And, all of those thoughts are just illusions. You know they are illusions because you wouldn't be thinking them if the essence of who you are wasn't just bursting at the seams to get out! You don't need objections if you're not being sold something! The essence of who you are is screaming to get out and another part of you is coming back with objections. "They can do it, but I can't", "They're smarter than me", "They're more educated than me", "They have start-up money, I don't have any." All of those are objections to a sales pitch that is constantly going on inside of you telling you that you can be happy, that life can be easy, and that you can give life purpose and meaning. Objections only come up as a rebuttal essentially saying "I'm scared of something, so I'm questioning the offer being made."

All the needs in Maslow's Hierarchy of needs are your needs! And if they are needs, then you can have them!!! You can get what you need. You can have even more than just your needs, but understand that they are there for every human being, not just the privileged. So often in history we hear of the self-actualized and they were the down trodden

Business Ownership Mindset

and the opposite of privileged.

We have to express who we are internally, because if we don't, we shut down. We become angry. We become bitter. We start to self-destruct. We start to do all sorts of stupid things that just hurt ourselves and others. And, the long term ramifications aren't worth the problem. And, the problem is that while we're going through this time of suppression, we don't see that it's a problem. We say things such as, "Oh I'll live", "At least I'm bringing in some money."

And, we don't see the long term ramifications; the loss of the house, the bankruptcy, and the whatever, because we didn't consciously create whatever it was that we needed to create in order to self-actualize. We need to be able to get in touch with whatever 'that' is, that we want, and be able to at least set up a plan that comes with, "Ok, I may not be able to do it right now, but I'll start up a plan for five years from now, and I'll make a five year transition plan that can start right now." At least then, that consciousness has somewhere to start growing and it's like letting pressure off a pressure cooker. Slowly is good. You don't have to let the pressure off right away. It's most important to be addressing it.

I just want to make sure you heard that clearly. I did not say, I'll make a plan and start it in five years. I said I'll create a plan, that may take me five years to bring to fruition but I'll start the building now. In other words; it may take me five years to build this building I see in my mind, and I have an idea of what I want the blueprints to look like, so I'll start today by checking out potential land, and maybe even an architect and I'll do something today and every day for the next five years so that five years from today, I'll have my building built. Or, in the world of business; I really want to run a company selling pens, but I can't see that happening for five years. If I create a plan that allows me to run a pen company in five years, I think having three years of pen sales experience first would be a great idea, and before that I could get a job doing what I do now in a pen company for a couple of years, so today I could start

Business Ownership Mindset

looking for a job in a pen company. (Ok, I'm not saying this is a great plan, or a speedy plan, but it's a five year plan that someone could start today. Who knows what kind of challenges my pen tycoon is facing right now?)

Business Ownership Mindset

3. How do we self-actualize?

    This is where the fun stuff starts to happen. This is where the passion in you starts happening and it's taking form. In being able to identify that there is always some 'thing' that somebody loves to do. It might not be their occupation. It might not be their job, but they love do it! Maybe they love going out painting, or they love going out for motorcycle rides, or they love petting their dog. Whatever 'it' is there is always some 'thing' that they love doing, but that they don't necessarily dedicate enough time to.

    Great. So, now for you, start figuring out what that 'thing' is, or at least the feeling that you get from 'that'. What else might you be able to get that feeling from? It might not be that you become a professional painter, or pro motorcycle driver or pet companion, but how do you take that feeling and start asking yourself, "If I could do anything, what might it be?"

"If I could do something with my business and transform it, what might that look like?"

    "How could I get that feeling from my transformation in my company?"

    Now you start brainstorming beyond the limits of what is and what could be and go, "You know what? Let's bring our pets to work!" or "Let's start having a paint shop at work."

    Whatever it is might seem ridiculous, but all of a sudden you start giving yourself permission to get that feeling not only in that one minute once a week, where it's "appropriate." But now it's, "How do I do that consistently?"

    Now you make a decision to bring yourself up, because when you're up, everybody benefits. When you're happy those around you have a chance to be happy. Like the saying, "When momma's happy,

Business Ownership Mindset

everybody's happy."

It starts with you. You've got to figure out for you what that is. And, I know, the problem in this book is going to be convincing autocrats that having fun is more productive than not having fun. And, I have the examples of managers giving their people movie passes for jobs well done and they got flak from the executive saying, "You're just softening them up. They're just going to be fluff."

Interestingly enough, that executive didn't realize he was just brining his own world view into the office and he didn't look objectively and the increase in productivity that was happening. I get it. There are some people who have already bought into this, and others who have not. This is why I'm writing the book! So that if you haven't bought into this already that you can start to question, what if I did do something different and it worked? Maybe even just for me. Remember, if momma's happy, everyone's happy. ;)

Maybe this is a good time to mention that we learn much faster and much easier when we're in a positive state of mind. Unlike in school when many of us were told that if we hunkered down, focused and had the threat of getting the strap (which some young people are wondering, "What does that mean???") was when we started to learn. Well that may have has some validity to it, but only because we didn't want to learn it! We wanted to be out playing soccer; we wanted to be out skipping rope, we didn't want to be in here doing this thing. But, when we were playing soccer nobody needed to beat us with a stick to learn how to run faster, or play harder or beat the other kid to the ball. We did that because it was fun and exciting! If it's something that you love to do, you don't have to hunker down and do it. Working hard is just 'working hard'. It's simply not working smarter or better so that you can be more successful. From a purely entertainment standpoint, you can pick out the successful people in your office, or other successful people around you, and ask them if they're involved in any physical activity that they enjoy, see if

Business Ownership Mindset

there seems to be a correlation. And then, ask those people who said yes, if they notice that it's easier to excel at a sport that they enjoy or one that is strict in its requirements.

One thing I've learned watching talented successful people, when their asked, how did you become successful? They've often answered with something to the effect of, "a lot of hard work" and I'd like to dissect that here. I don't believe that success comes with "hard work". I believe it comes with perseverance and tenacity. I believe it comes with endurance training and tendering. I believe it comes with a lot of things that from the outside, and sometimes even the inside look like "hard work". But, my problem with the notion of "hard work" is that it's "hard". And no, I'm not lazy. And, yes I do like it when things are easy. However, I know that hard work for the sake of being hard does not create success. Yes, sometimes you won't want to practice, and yes sometimes it is boring, and yes I get it you don't like doing that thing, but doing it doesn't mean it's "hard", nor does making an easy task hard make you more prone to success by doing it.

Get it out of your head that mastering a skill, even if that skill is running a wildly profitable company, has to be hard. It does not. Yes, it may take longer than you think it should have. In fact I almost guarantee that one. And, you may find yourself doing a lot of things that you don't like doing. And, you may find yourself sucking wind at doing somethings. Ok, so what? You weren't that good at riding a bike when you first learned how either. And, your friends might think you're a dork working on a Friday night instead of going out with them. Friends don't tend to like change; it's their job to challenge you. All of this, I call tempering. Just like iron in the fire and under the hammer, we too will be tempered. And, we will become stronger, and smarter and more skilled because of it. Its job is to help us let go of our resistance. Resistance is temporary, it's a part of life and living, but we don't have to succumb to it. In fact, in order to self-actualize we need to break through it and shed it. A friend of

Business Ownership Mindset

mine, Stefan Arnio, says "Respect the grind".

So, how do we self-actualize? Find the thing you love to do, and find a way to master it. Go through every level of awareness from mass awareness to mastery*, and do it over and over again with everything you love until the day you die. It might be one thing. It might be more things that you can remember. That's irrelevant. It's about going after the things that move you, because it moves you.

*Levels of Awareness are covered more in Chapter 7 – 5

Business Ownership Mindset

Chapter 4
Enlightenment through Business

In order to fully express ourselves, I don't believe that it is enough to master our skills and sell them at an hourly rate. In order to become all that we can become, to let go of our resistance and conditioning that we learned growing up, that hid us from the truth of who we are, we need to find a way to bring those skills to the world with no fear, no protection and no security blanket. It's being able to say, "Hey world, here I am. How do you like me now?" and, to not be emotionally attached to that answer. It's being IN THE ZONE.

1. <u>It brings up our resistance.</u>

Being in business brings up our resistance. Even the most veteran serial entrepreneur that's jazzed and excited about running another business will have some resistance come up, not necessarily immediately but as they are running the business. It brings up the things that stall us. It brings up the things that which we're afraid of, it brings up our limiting beliefs, it brings up everything that is hostile and not going right in our lives, it brings up our prudence and it brings up the lines we're willing to cross and the lines we're not willing to cross. It brings up our risk tolerance and it brings up our self-assurance. We're hitting that boundary of our comfort zone and at that boundary are all of our emotional barbed wire fences and all of our defences; our limits are all right there.

Now, what resistance is, how it shows up in our lives, and how we go beyond it; I'll touch on again in upcoming parts of the book. But, it's important to understand here, that you can't be in business without having your resistance brought up. You can neither be growing,

Business Ownership Mindset

stagnating, nor be closing down a business, without having your resistance being brought up. The good of that statement, though, is that through the process of being in business you are constantly going to be going through the tempering process. And, the good part of that is that you are continually strengthening yourself and building your competence, your character, and your wealth of experience.

Business Ownership Mindset

2. What is resistance?

What is resistance? Is it fear? Yes. But, it's also everything and anything that stops us from getting to do what we want to do in a moment. What I mean by 'what I want to do' is anything that moves us closer toward our goals. So, even feeling tired and saying, "I don't feel like it" is a form of resistance.

Innately we all want to create. We all have this 'thing' that I talked about in chapter 1, where, "I want to be able to express myself." Therefore, anything that stops us from being able to express ourselves fully, I call resistance.

Now understand that at one point in time the idea that now holds us back might have worked for us. You know when we were five and mom said, "Don't cross the street without holding my hand." It made sense. We were too short to see over the hood of the parked car and the drivers couldn't see us either. But when we reach 35, 36, ok 40 I'll give you that, you have to be able to cross the street by yourself without holding mom's hand. But, if you still hold onto that belief that says, "It's not safe to cross the street without holding someone's hand," it may not be that you think you literally need to hold someone's hand, but it might be that there's a huge amount of fear crossing the street. It may even be irrational to you and you don't know why it is there. You know you're safe, you know you're big enough to be seen, but you still have this trepidation crossing the street. That in its self is resistance. It comes up in many different forms. This example is simply an example, but all resistance is created in a similar fashion, in that it was useful at one point in time, but it no longer serves us.

I've been asked, "Is resistance fear based, or is it risk based?" In other words if I were to ask myself if I wanted to merge my company with another but the risk doesn't seem to be worth it, is that still defined as resistance? What distinguishes me from stepping out of my comfort zone

Business Ownership Mindset

and investing in something for example, which I know is a risky venture, versus me taking a risk at something that I've never done before, but I know that the possibilities are grand? How do you differentiate between something that is fear based and something that is just prudent and risk based?"

The answer is that I don't differentiate. To me, prudence is fear based. And, I say that because we are taught that unless we have all our ducks in a row before we start something that we're not allowed to start it. If we take, for example, someone who is highly analytical. They're going to have a whole lot more prudence and a whole lot more rules around what it takes for them to move forward on a decision, and their fear is justified. "I don't want my bridges to fall down", "I don't want anybody to die", it's justified and it makes sense. Until it doesn't.

That prudence or that fear, I'm ok with it in that circumstance because you want to have that! But, I don't differentiate between the two. So, let's go back to the idea that it makes sense until it doesn't. As long as that prudence, I'll call it fear, keeps that engineer building safe bridges and coming up with new and creative ways to build bridges that withstand the forces that are lambasted upon it, then the fear is useful and it makes sense to justify it as prudence. It doesn't inhibit the engineer from building, creating and being creative. But! As soon as it starts to creep in and stop the creativity, or stop the growth process, then it becomes resistance. Just like you have resistance in an electrical wire, the resistance stops the energy from travelling to the light filament and the light is dim; dimmer than it could be. Without the resistance the light can shine brighter! Now I'm going to get the electrical engineer saying, "Yes, but if you reduce your resistance and allow more energy through you burn out the filament faster and you have NO light." This brings us back to, "It works, until it doesn't work." There's a fine line that we walk between safety and risk. And if we walk too far on the side of safety then we don't allow for the full potential that exists in the system.

Business Ownership Mindset

3. How does Resistance show up?

Resistance shows up in a myriad of different ways.

Imagine yourself in your office. Life is going tickety boo when all of a sudden someone starts yelling at you for no reason. Now, if you work at home alone this would be extremely bizarre, and if you work with a relatively sane group of people this may be unheard of, and if you work with a group of people where this is an hourly happenstance then you might not even notice. However, regardless of your circumstances the odds are fairly good that you're going to have some emotional walls come up. These emotional walls are meant to defend you, to take care of you. They tell the offending person that as long as they stay on their side of the wall, that you will stay on your side of the wall and that no one will get hurt if you stick to your perspective side of the wall.

The problem with this, of course, is that there are no real walls. Most people don't see this happening and what ensues from here is anyone's guess. Well, not really. What happens from here on is actually quite predictable because you will have a habit of dealing with things "like this" in a particular manner, and however you deal with it, your antagonist will have their habit of how they deal with your reaction.

Let's look at the way you would deal with this. You're presumably in an office, drinking a warm cup of your favorite daily beverage, when suddenly someone starts freaking out on you. It could be a co-worker, a disgruntled client or the like. Now think about the way you think you'd react. Now think of the way you'd actually likely react. You may think you would remain calm and objective, but it's more likely that your adrenalin is going to hit, your heart is going to speed up and then you're going to do what you do when that happens. Do you assess the situation, relax and deal with it logically? Depending on who it is do you recognize them and think, "Not this again..." or do lash out and fight back? All of these can be

Business Ownership Mindset

forms of resistance depending on whether or not it moves us toward our goal. Anyone of these could be a conscious choice depending on whether or not we're thinking through how we're going to respond this time.

Some people who are afraid of conflict will immediately go into calm rescuing mode, some people who are intolerant of others drama may tune it out and ignore it immediately and some people who are charged up by conflict might immediately jump into it to shut it down. All of which are forms of resistance.

Any reaction that we have which takes us out of the immediate circumstances and into a response based on past events is really resistance. Now we can't be assessing every single reaction we have to every single thing we do in a day because that would be exhausting not to mention futile. The question has to be, "Is this, my behaviour, getting me closer to my goal or not?" If it is, keep doing it. If it's not, then we want to look at it and change it.

How do we know the difference between resistance and responding? Resistance tends to be more of an immediate response; more of a reaction if you will. Responding requires the ability to see the situation as it is and neither attack it, defend it nor move away from it. If your reaction to the situation is more emotional that neutral then you're likely reacting to the situation and not responding to it.

There are many forms of resistance. Some are more subtle than others. If you've ever been in a class room and tuned the teacher out, to the point where they sound like the teacher in a Peanut's cartoon, "Meh meh meh meh, meh met meh met," then you've experienced resistance. In that moment you weren't present to the world around you, you were either reminiscing about the past or day dreaming about the future, but you weren't IN the moment. That is a form of resistance. Any time we take ourselves out of the present moment, or as I like to say, "Anytime we take ourselves out of the game..." we're in resistance.

Business Ownership Mindset

4. How do we let go of it?

There are essentially three ways that we change our beliefs, and resistance is simply a lot of beliefs that we have all in agreements saying, "Don't go there!" So if we want to change our beliefs that are slowing us down from moving ahead, we're going to implement one of these three concepts.

1. Reason,
2. Repetition and
3. Emotional charge.

Let's look at REASON. When we become aware of the ideas that we believe, most of the time we can rationally look at it and decide if we want to keep thinking this particular way or not. We might say something and then be shocked that we said it and think, "Where did that come from?" Maybe it was something racist, or sexist, or we suddenly said something to our kids that our parents used to say to us. Whatever it is, we know it's out of character for us and we can easily look at the comment objectively and think, "That's not me. I don't agree with that." And if we contemplate it past that, we can actually decide right then and there to change that programing in our mind and say, "That sounds like mom, I don't think that and I'm not going to say that again." And we don't! The idea has been reasoned with, a decision has been made and the commitment to the new way of thinking will effortlessly be followed through on. It can happen that easily. It does happen that easily! And, I encourage you to do it all day long. As a growing influencer, you will get in the habit of changing your beliefs often because you'll see that what worked for you in one circumstance doesn't work in all circumstances and you need to be flexible in finding out what does work in the new circumstances that you find yourself in and you need to be willing to go with it. (Changing beliefs and changing decisions are NOT the same thing.)

Business Ownership Mindset

The more you learn to change your beliefs, the faster and easier it will happen and eventually, ideally, all of your changes in beliefs will simply happen through reason.

But, as we all know, it doesn't always happen that easily. You'll need to employ different methods to change more engrained beliefs. And by engrained beliefs, I mean that an idea is tied into a multitude of other beliefs. It's not a simple black and white choice of, "It's either this or that or both", there's actually more tied to the belief that makes it more complex.

Not only will you employ this for yourself, but as an influencer of the masses, you'll likely be more involved in this and the third method than you ever were in the first, whether it's in one on one conversations, speeches, or marketing; repetition and emotional charge will be far more effective than simply reason. But of course, you already know that. ;)

By 'this', I'm referring to REPETITION. As part of our brains function, when we hear something often enough eventually we will believe it, whether it's true or not, whether it's supportive or not, and whether it's right or not, that's irrelevant, eventually we will believe it.

Repetition is the foundation of dogma, it's the foundation of parenting, and it's the foundation of marketing. It's the foundation of these things because it works. And the good news is that it'll work for you too! Self-imposed repetition is just as, if not in some cases more, effective than external repetition. Whomever we perceive to have the "authority" to dictate to us, will win.

I'm sure you've heard the expression most sales people are taught, "If you say it, it's questionable, but if the client says it, it's true." The reasoning behind this is that when I as in individual say something, I'm saying it because I believe it. And, OBVIOUSLY, if I believe it, it's true!! (She says with a note of sarcasm)

Consequently, if you say something often enough, eventually

Business Ownership Mindset

you'll believe it. The question then arises, "How long is eventually?" And we don't know the answer to that. If something is said stoically, without emotion, and the statement contradicts something that is very emotionally engrained in an individual, eventually could seem to take a lifetime. Needless to say, we'd like to speed that up significantly. So what do we do? We add in elixir number 3; emotional charge.

EMOTIONAL CHARGE is responsible for every core belief you have, every childhood belief you have, and every deeply engrained belief that you have. How do I know that? It's simple. Emotion by definition is simply an intensification of thought. So, what was once rational, added in with numerous other thoughts and reinforced, now becomes emotional.

As children until the age of reason, around 7-9 we are little balls of emotion. Every thought is intense and every action is intense. We live hard and we sleep hard. Nothing we do then is done in a mediocre sense of unimportance. It can seem crazy to us that as an adult we will still hold on to beliefs with such intensity, especially beliefs that seem inconsequential or undefended and lacking evidence. But, as a child, it absolutely is consequential and it is evidence based! Even if that evidence or consequence is only potential in nature! Let me give you an example. Let's go back to our earlier example of the executive that had a fear of walking across the street alone. As an adult he had an irrational fear of crossing the street, but when we traced back the origin of that fear, we found out that as a child crossing the road that he developed that trigger and reaction. It was because he was the youngest boy of four and nearly every time he crossed the street with his mother as a young boy his mother would take his hand in hers and while crossing the street she was attempting to keep track of the other three boys, who inevitably would run across the street not look for cars, she would panic. That panic in mom was felt by the young boy holding his mom's hand, even though he at the time was in no danger and he knew it.

It wasn't that there was any trauma, nothing bad ever happened.

Business Ownership Mindset

It was simply the emotional charge of mom, being felt by the boy who, by experience, created a belief that elicited panic when crossing the street.

I'm sure I have a bazillion more examples of that, but more importantly you want to understand that there are times when you have an emotional charge around beliefs that are perfectly logical.

For example, sticking with the theme, and hopefully you'll catch the metaphor; you could be afraid of crossing the street because you walked across the street and got hit by a car. That's an emotional response to an emotional event and it's totally rational as to why the emotional charge is there.

You could be afraid of crossing the street because you were told to be afraid of crossing the street without an adult around so many times that you bought into it.

You could be afraid of crossing the street because you were with someone who was afraid of your safety, their safety, someone else's safety, or someone else's previous unsafety.

My point is this; as a child we create 'beliefs', 'triggers', 'if/then statements', call them what you will...we create them through emotional charge because life at that time was an emotional charge, and not necessarily because it was traumatic, significant or consequential. And, when it comes to changing our beliefs that are emotional, sometimes reason or repetition won't be significant enough to change those beliefs and we'll need to identify the source in order to use that emotion "against itself" to change it to a new belief. Once we've found that initial sensitizing event, reason may indeed be enough to change the belief. And, there are numerous methods of being able to do this. I of course recommend Success Therapy. We can change in a two hour session what might otherwise take years or decades to change.

We'll talk about that more later.

Business Ownership Mindset

Know this; our memories are perfect although our ability to recall it may be questionable. We wouldn't know how to say "hello" if the memories of having learned how to say hello, what it meant, when to say it and who to say it to wasn't engrained in our memory. The more we say hello, to the same kind of people in the same kind of situations, the more those memories are enforced and ingrained and the easier it is to say without having to look back upon the memory. But, the fundamentals with which we learned it are still very much intact.

The same thing holds true with EVERYTHING we think, know or believe. If you want to know why you believe what you believe, the answer is in your past. Whether it's personal, in business, in fear or in trust, the reason that you believe what you believe is in your past. If you can rationally think a different way knowing new information, do that all day long! If that doesn't work, look at repetition and if that's not working follow the emotional charge, it's like an electrical wire, your mind will take you there.

Oh by the way; because we have a rational aspect to our mind and a metaphorical aspect to our mind, left and right brains you might say, you don't need to know the exact happenstance of why you think the way you do. So if you find yourself trying to unravel those proverbial Christmas lights of knotted wiring in your mind and all that comes up is mish mash, breathe and relax there are methods for letting go of that too. Sometimes it can be as easy as thinking, "What would I like to do with this mish mash?", "Throw it out and buy another set of lights." Done! Picture it happening. And lo and behold, the thoughts can change.

The concepts covered in this subchapter are the topic of discussions in entire fields of study. Don't think you need to know it all nor that you do know it all. But, if you have more questions than answers from this section please visit us at www.MySuccessTherapy.com and we'll be happy to share some leading edge resources with you.

Business Ownership Mindset

5. How it happens; an evolutionary process

As we move up the entrepreneurial ladder we will naturally embrace our innate passion. You're naturally going to focus on your strengths because you'll have a tendency to spend your time doing the things that you love to do and you'll be recognized for the things that you do well.

In my case I was recognized for being a great shit disturber and it lead me up the quick start to business path. Hahaha...

As I mentioned earlier, going into business is a tendering process. When we go through these changes in positions we are taking on greater and greater self-responsibility. And, by taking on those greater self-responsibilities, we have to shed and let go of our inadequacies. We have to let go of our weaknesses, we have to let go of that fear, that shyness, that whatever it is that holds us back from moving into the next phase. We're drawn into a world where we no longer give a great amount of negative attention to the things we don't do well, but rather take that force or energy and put it into the things we do well.

If we put a consorted effort into succeeding as quickly as possible we gain an understanding of the things we don't do well rather than fear it, we understand well enough to delegate it to someone else so that we haven't lost control of it or avoided control of it, but rather we take complete control over it, by intentionally placing it in the hands of someone competent and we know they're competent because we know it well enough to know the difference between competent and smoke, but not necessarily much more than that.

Eventually, if we're not there already, we get to a point where we're not really in it for the money. Well we are, but...it's like a friend of mine puts it, "We love it so much we'd do it for free, but we're so good at it that we charge a lot."

Business Ownership Mindset

Even great CEOs will know their passion and follow it like an arrow. They walk into a job, not because they need the money, but because they know their passion. They walk into a new company thinking, "I can turn this place around!" and they love the thrill of it, the excitement that it brings to them. But, I assure you, to get to that point, they've shed a ton, if not a tonne, of fear and limiting beliefs.

To fast pace this, allow yourself to be driven by your passion, face your fears and let go of them.

Now, this is not to say that CEO's never experience fear. Haha! Yes, yes they do. They too are human. However, the more they understand, consciously or simply live into the idea, unconsciously that every rung of the corporate ladder requires a different mindset, the more adapt they are to succeeding in the new role. They know that what made them successful at one rung, might be the death of their career in another rung. And, that they may need to let go of certain beliefs in order to succeed in their new role.

The CEO who is still trying to make everyone happy, will not succeed as CEO for long, not because they aren't a competent CEO, but because they'll stress themselves out of a position in the company, even if it's their own company. It's the ambiguity in their mind that will tear them down, regardless of their degree of skill.

In order to succeed as the CEO of your own company, you must let go of certain mindsets and embrace a whole new set that will be completely foreign to you. You may love them! You might embrace them with a whole new level of passion, but they are not common place in world of employee, sales, management, or solo entrepreneur.

Business Ownership Mindset

6. For the good of all mankind or just the shareholders

Let's look at the thesis that your thoughts create your reality and how to transform fear and risk though passion. The following is a question brought forth during a conversation on resistance in business.

Q: Michelle let's reconcile the fact that you may now have this fork in the road. You have two options at least and you know that the trajectory that you're on right now, you've brought it on to you. Now if you take the riskier road that you feel passionate about, we have to see how to create that reality. Say you see something you perceive as grander as serving society. If what you have is a riskless adventure but it doesn't serve society it just serves the shareholders, and where you want to go is riskier but it serves society. Let's take Apple. (No one in this conversation works with Apple. Apple did not even know we had this conversation about them, if they're offended my apologies.) They went down the path with the iphone. (No one in this conversation works with Microsoft either. Microsoft did not even know we had this conversation even though it wasn't about them, and if they're offended, my apologies. Just making sure they don't feel left out.) It's a service based commodity and look what it did for Apple. So they had a vision that they wanted to serve people and take the risky venture…(implied question.)

Michelle: Ok, let's look at the big picture. Let's look at Coca-Cola. (No one in this conversation works with Coca-Cola. Coca-Cola did not even know we had this conversation about them, and if they're offended, my apologies.) They can say, "We want to bring water to the world." But we all know that their commitment is to their shareholders.

Q: What do you mean by that?

Michelle: Meaning that they decided that they were going to bring Coke to Africa, they brought their whole line up to 3rd world countries around the globe. Coke-Cola has a line of water that they bottle

Business Ownership Mindset

and distribute and it's available all over the world. They bring coke and all their other lines of beverages all over the world. It's slathered across Africa. If you perceive sugared beverages as being unhealthy, then it might even be better that Coke-Cola is responsible to their shareholders saying, "No, we're not going to go into this part of the world because there's no money in it."

Q: The question here is the distinguishing need to help others. They're smart they have their teams of people figuring out what's going to sell, bring in health drinks into schools. Very quickly they saw the trend and started investing money into the health platform. They were just following the people, the market. The distinguishing factor in here is to say you can let the people lead your market, which is what everybody does. "Where's my market going? That's where I want to be."

Or you can say, "Where should the market be?"

In this consciousness based world. Are you the kind of CEO that wants to create consciousness? That wants to create a better world? Then you need to take the market where it needs to be. Or, are you the kind of CEO that just wants to make money and asks where's the market going and you go there. One is the enlightened CEO who goes against the grain because he's coming from a heart centred perspective and the other one is enlightened enough to know, "I want to know where the market is going, not just where it is, but I think there"

Michelle: Let's get back into the mindset of the successful business owner. The truth is you're going to have to be focused on both. Business can't survive if it's not attentive to revenue, and likewise it won't survive long if the owner isn't attentive to their passion. I'd bet nickels to dimes that Apple closed all their R&D outside of iphones because of the revenue, profit and feasibility of focusing on one product. I'd also bet that they chose phones because it represented the largest untapped market. And thirdly, I'd venture to say that iphone became the computer/user

Business Ownership Mindset

intense device that it is because of the passion that Apple and Steve Jobs had around creating a device that people could use everywhere at any time. There has to be a balance. If you're not in business to create revenue then you've bought yourself a job. And if you really don't focus on revenue you've started a bankrupt company, it's just a matter of time. But when you see how to build your passion into a revenue generating machine, then you have something magical.

Business Ownership Mindset

7. Business is the best personal development training

In my opinion there is no better way of being able to figure out who you are and what you're made of, how creative you can get, how ingenuitive you can get than to go into business for yourself. And whether it's through necessity and fear or passion and an "I get to" attitude, it will happen anyway. It's like the expression, "All roads lead to Rome", it doesn't matter how you get there, but that's where you're going.

There's a story of a CEO who would walk around and just talk to people in the organization, everyone from the janitor to the admin assistants. This CEO would pick up nuggets of wisdom from everyone and apply the information that would improve the organization and their objectives. Because of that personability the staff was willing to speak openly. When this happens out of confidence and not fear, the result is explosive growth. This CEO didn't NEED to get information from the staff. There was a conscious choice to hear the voices of those in the know and decide from there what information brought them cohesively or collectively toward the goals of the company and, ultimately of course, the CEO.

It becomes not about only listening to your immediate circle or the ones that you think are "good enough" to contribute, but in understanding that everyone has value to contribute to the greater good. It's about creating connections with the intention of growth as individuals and as a company. It doesn't matter who you are. Normally our hierarchical perspective says, "I'll only talk to my executives, I don't talk to you. If you have an issue, go through the appropriate channels."

Don't get me wrong, there's a time and a place for going through the appropriate channels, but from a personal development training ground of the CEO perspective, be willing to see the value in everyone and

Business Ownership Mindset

be willing to act on brilliant information that moves you closer to your goals regardless of who it comes from. It'll speed up your success.

Business Ownership Mindset

Chapter 5
Rules of the game as employee through to BOM
And why they aren't transferable

I've seen it time and time again where people think that because they succeeded as an employee that they have everything it takes to succeed as a business owner, and that's simply not true. It requires an entirely different mindset that has to be there to succeed in the new position. For example, as an employee one is always trying to please their boss, because if they do what their boss wants done right, then they get to keep their job and life is good. When it comes to ones clients though, as a business owner, one can't necessarily think that they have to do whatever the clients want them to do and that it's going to work, because it's not. It's going to backfire more often than not and the business owner is going to end up getting themselves into so much trouble that they don't know what to do with themselves. They might find themselves overpromising on things they can't deliver on or they might not be standing up for themselves. They have to learn how to stand up for themselves, even as sales people, to be successful in their occupation.

The other thing is that as a higher end sales person, they not only have to be able to stand up for themselves, their decisions and what's going on around them, but in certain situations, such as if they're going to be meeting with the CEO of a company, in order to be able to do their job, they're going to have to be able to create rapport with them. In order to be able to create rapport with executives, they have to be able to not turtle every time they're asked something. If they do turtle, then they haven't created rapport, the executive is not going to like the sales rep, they're not going to trust them and they're not going to want to deal with

Business Ownership Mindset

that person at all.

The whole rule of engagement as an employee is almost on its head as a sales person. There is a complete contradiction from what it takes to be successful as an employee to being a successful sales person; and likewise from a salesperson to an entrepreneur.

As a sales person I may use the premise that the client's always right to see how I might be able to improve on this situation and I'll take your complaint and I'll see what I can do with it. As an entrepreneur I can't always be doing that. I have to be able to have the mindset of, "You know what? I'm running my business like 'this'. If you'd like it run like 'that', that's awesome but you'd probably be better off dealing with so and so down the street. And, you know what? It's ok for you to leave. I don't need the business." You probably don't want to use those exact words with your outside voice to the client, but absolutely have the attitude.

A successful sales person needs to know that they don't need that particular sale in order to succeed because feeling desperate for a sale leads to self-sabotage. But, for the most part, the job of a sales person is to figure out how to make things work out. For a sales person to walk away from potential business seems asinine. They'd be screaming, "Are you on crack!??! How can we not resolve this issue?" As a business owner, I have to be able to say, "This doesn't fit in my paradigm. I know what I want. This is what we do and this is all we do. Everything else has to go." Imagine a company like Ferrari bowing down to a potential customer who says, "I want it cheaper." It's not going to happen. People who want a cheaper sports car don't shop at Ferrari and everyone knows it.

There's a motivation factor here. The business person can say, "That's not my passion. I know I can make a lot of money without this. You can go over there. " It's not completely unlike the enlightened sales person who will say, "I know you want to buy a gazillion dollars' worth of

Business Ownership Mindset

our stuff, but you really don't need it." Neither one is motivated strictly by the money. This is where the beliefs driving the motivation comes in.

The sales person doesn't necessarily have the cost side of the equation. They'll get the contract signed to get the deal, which is after all their job. The cost portion is borne by the overhead of the company and there are no consequences to this person (Immediately).

As an entrepreneur, if you're making a decision based on money alone, and your decision isn't passion based, you'll do the job if in the end you can make a profit. That kind of thinking won't last long, because the consequences to the company are always consequences to the entrepreneur and ALL costs will be considered in future dealing or at some point. Stress, aggravation, distraction from the main objection all have a cost attached to them. Ignored, that added cost can take a company down.

If you want to be successful as an entrepreneur you need to identify 'this' is your passion, 'this' is what you want to do, and you're going to stick to it. Without that, people tend to do a lot of things that bring them down. If they get to a pressure cooker point where they're doing a whole ton of stuff that they don't like doing and it's not 'them', then really all they've done is made themselves an employee to their clients. And that's why that mentality isn't transferable.

In all successful endeavours you'll want to find the thing you love to do, aim for it and take action on it. Excel with where you're at and take on the roles and duties of the next level that you aspire towards. That aspect is universal. However some of the rules of the game are different at each level.

Business Ownership Mindset

1. **<u>Succeeding as an Employee</u>**

You have to be willing to take direction from people and follow through on it. Yes, there are jobs and positions where initiative thinking is encouraged and rewarded, but for the most part it has the same requirements as school. Listen to your boss and do what they say. If feedback is given, look at it, ask how you can improve and do what it takes to improve.

See chapter 1 to review the bullet points.

Business Ownership Mindset

2. <u>Succeeding as a Sales Rep</u>

This is where you have to start taking initiative. You need to be self-directed and you need to learn to not take things personally. You need to learn to work on your own as the lone leader. You need to look at feedback and question whether or not it will help you to achieve your goals, and if not then let it go.

There's a freedom that comes with being in sales. You get to manage your own time. You get to manage your own behaviours and you get to manage how you orchestrate your days. With this freedom comes the different mindset that I've been referring to. Now with managing your own time, you need to honour your choices and learn to stick to them. If you decide that 9am is prospecting time, then at 9am you need to be prospecting. That means not bowing down to the needs of your client that call at 8:55 in a panic and need your help. How are you going to choose to handle this? Like an employee or like a sales person? If that 9am time slot was with the CEO of Coke-Cola, would you call and reschedule to deal with your current client's crisis? Or would you schedule another time to deal with it? Does it depend on the crisis? Or does it depend on something else? Does it depend on whether it's the first time this week that it's happened or if it's the third time?

All of these questions are common place for any sales person. Clients will call in with problems. I guarantee it. And I guarantee that if you're still dealing with it with the mindset of an employee, you're going to go broke. You need to honour your time and ensure that you've blocked off enough of it to do revenue generating activity to keep you on track to achieving your goals.

Now, this doesn't mean that you ignore your clients concerns. That too is a recipe for disaster. Conflict avoidance is a death trap for a sales person. You need to learn or begin learning the skills of influence.

Business Ownership Mindset

3. Succeeding as a Manager

Whether you choose to be a micro manager, a macro manager, or somewhere in between management requires letting go of being the "technician". You're not the one doing the job anymore. For some people building on people's strengths and teaching others how to succeed is the hardest part of this job. For some people learning to give direction and sharing their knowledge with the team is the hardest part, especially if transitioning from sales or other 'lone' positions.

Good management requires learning how to take responsibility for other people's actions knowing that they are key influencers and they have the ability to respond to all situations under their direction. As I mentioned earlier, management is about letting go of how it gets done and making sure that it gets done. It's being in charge, but leading the team. It's setting people up for success, allowing for learning but still meeting the standards of the company. It's definitely a balancing act.

Business Ownership Mindset

4. **<u>Succeeding as an Entrepreneur</u>**

Entrepreneurs need to take self-direction to a whole new level. Not only are they in charge of their own schedules, their own marketing choices, their own sales choices, their own revenue choices, their own product choices, but they are in fact in charge of every choice made in a company on a daily basis. They need to see themselves as decision makers. And, they need to see themselves as go getters. They're also the ones who get everything done that they said they would do. They need to be willing to go off the beaten path and do things differently than everyone around them. They need to not only be lone wolves, but even to the point of renegade, or rebel. They need to be willing to not fit in with anyone. (No that doesn't mean you don't have any friends.)

Let's break it all down because to say that someone needs to be a leader, doesn't give anyone enough direction to lead. Much to the grimace of most entrepreneurs their coaches or mentors will first ask them, "What do you want?" Whether it's what do you want to create in your business? What do you want to achieve? What are your one year, five year, ten year, and twenty year goals? Some variation on, "What do you want?" is going to be the first thing you need to know. And, whether you have an inkling of an idea, such as I want to be a consultant, or you have a full blown business model with projections and organizational charts, you still need to create a vision and run with it. We'll get into how to do this in a later section of the book.

An underlying aspect of knowing what you want is that you may not really KNOW what you want. But as Napoleon Hill wrote in 1938, and it's been proven true ever since, millionaires of his time and this one, make decisions quickly and change their minds slowly, if at all. He goes on to write that they run the risk of being obstinate but obstinate is much more preferential to not being able to make a decision or changing it too frequently. To get in the habit of knowing what you want, even if you

Business Ownership Mindset

don't know, you need to be able to throw the proverbial dart at the map, call that your decision and aim for it. What I'm referring to here is an attitude or a way of thinking that precludes the actual decision being made, and whether it's the "right" decision or not.

Entrepreneurship requires an independent train of thought, a willingness to do things the way you want to because you want to. It's that willingness to follow your heart and find your dreams because you can. It's knowing that you're safe because you are. You are resourceful and you'll find a way. It's knowing that you're part of a bigger calling even if you're not surrounded by friends yet. It's knowing that you can find out how even if you totally don't know how, and you don't need to know how, yet. You'll figure out how after you find out what works. It's curiosity and a willingness to experiment and find things out. It's about owning your destiny and taking control of your life.

Oh and don't worry if you haven't mastered all of those, or even any of those. This is why it's a journey! This is why some people step into and then go back to a job. (10 or 20 times) This is why it's mind boggling and challenging and infuriating sometimes. (more often than not) And, this is why it's so exciting and enticing.

Business Ownership Mindset

5. Succeeding as a Business Owner

You have to be able to say, "Ok I've built my baby up and now I need to be willing to let it go." You can't hold on to it anymore. You have to be willing to let your employees do their thing with it. You have to be willing to let go of it and figure out what to do because now your job is to go and strategize. Your job now is to be able to have time to go and talk to employees and figure out where you're at, and being able to spend time alone figuring out where you want to go from here. It's no longer about doing "the thing."

Going back to our child crossing the street example, you're now the adult. At what point in the development of the child do you let go?

Your staff is in a position where they make decisions involving hundreds of thousands of dollars, they buy houses, they make decisions on what school their child is going to, they make decisions on everything, are they supposed to set aside their intelligence when they come to work? No. You need to trust them. You'll set up boundaries within which to make those decisions, but at some point you need to trust them! You know you don't have a monopoly on how it's done. There are numerous ways to get the job done. Your job is no longer deciding how the job gets done; it's deciding THAT the job gets done. You've hired competent people to take care of the details and figure out how it's going to get done.

Without their creativity you're not creating a team. You need their creativity to create a synergy in order to create something that is bigger than yourself or even than the two of you exclusively. And really, how are you going to continue learning if you're only continuing to do what you already know?

Now more than ever, you'll also be the creative engine that directs the ship. You're the one with the vision of where you see the

Business Ownership Mindset

company going, the potential it has and see the path you're going to take to get you there. You can absolutely call on the genius of others, whether it's your executives, your board of directors, your coaches, your mentors, your mastermind peers or someone else. But, in the end all visionary decisions and communication of that vision lie in your hands.

Communication and the willingness to master this skill will also be paramount. You may find yourself drawing on a whole new set of skills in the department of creativity, strategy, and cultural dynamics; none of which were necessarily required as an entrepreneur; but are now all essential as a business owner.

The reason the skills you had as an employee aren't transferable to business ownership that as an employee fundamentally you had to position your focus of control in the company, as an entrepreneur that focus had to come back to you. As a Business Owner that focus of control still lies with you but now you need to let the day to day tasks be decided by someone else AND know that they depend on you for being their focus of control. As an employee you can't insist on pursuing your company vision; as the Business Owner, you HAVE to insist that everyone is pursuing your company vision. As an employee you have to get approval from your superiors before you act; as the Business Owner, you HAVE to be willing to not have any approval from your potential prospects, peers or anyone else for that matter. Throughout the book I will be driving home what it takes to be a successful Business Owner, and I understand that a lot of the ideas aren't going to be comfortable one's for you, nor will they be comforting to you. But, when you find yourself willing to let go of ideas that used to be safe and hone into the possibility that completely contradictory ideas will actually work better for you, then the doors of possibility will fly open for you!

Understand that thoughts create our reality. So when you ask yourself, "Where do I want to be?, Would I like to be where my passions lie?", you may say initially, "That doesn't bring me enough money." Ask if

Business Ownership Mindset

you're willing to find a way to have both your passion and find a way for it to bring in the money? If so, what might that look like? How might you get some help to see it blossom into something even better? Let me assure you that when your passions align with a solid business plan, fantastic things can happen.

Business Ownership Mindset

Chapter 6
How to fail in Business
(Don't evolve, stay the same)

1. <u>Other people's needs are more important.</u>

By the way, this is a good way to fail in life too. ;)

If I believe that other people's needs are more important than mine, then I'm actually more likely to fail at my business than if I meet my needs first. If I have a fear that client's going to leave me if I'm not at their beck and call, I run the risk spending my time putting out their fires at the expense of building my own business.

I am much better off if I just explain, "You know what, I can't meet you now, but I can meet you next week on Wednesday or sometime after that. If that's not good enough, sorry, but, it's going to have to be because that's the way it's going down." I have to be able to stand in that kind of integrity and say, "This is what's important to me", before their needs. (Unless of course you're a heart surgeon...Or a fireman!)

That's not what you say to someone, but that's the mindset you have to have. You need to take care of your own needs first and then consider others. Even if they've paid you to take care of theirs! If they pay you to be at your beck and call then they had best be paying you enough to warrant it. If a company pays more for a three hour return time, then make sure that what you charge them is enough to fulfil that AND to keep you in business. Otherwise, you're going to have to look at your set up and reassess what is a reasonable turnaround time with the resources you have, or what's a reasonable fee to get the resources you need to increase that turnaround time.

Business Ownership Mindset

The thing you can't do is offer them the moon when you don't have the moon to give them. You also can't put their needs ahead of your own.

Business Ownership Mindset

2. Caring what other people think; judgement.

Of course caring what other people think is important but it's more about listening to what other people have to say and then lining it up with your beliefs yourself. Yes people are judging you based on where you're going, but it's from the perspective that they see you moving. They may say things like, "Hey, I see where you're going and this is not the right way to go!" And that's what you really don't want to own.

People may say, "Wow, you're really like this." And if you're treated like "this", it's only because you believe you're like "this." When there's a part of you that believes it, it brings that to the surface where you look at it and say, "Yes, I believe 'this' about myself." For example if someone says you're going the wrong way and you buy into thinking you are indeed going the wrong way, then they have simply brought up your own self-doubt. What this person is saying verifies this belief and this feeling inside.

Whereas if I tell you the sky is green. You simply reply back and say, "No. Why would you say that?" Because you are convinced in the deepest root of your own experience that the sky is not green. It could be the person with the utmost authority telling you that the sky is green and you know it's not. But, if someone says you're not a successful business person and if there is a part of you that may have that belief, then you might start doubting yourself. So why can't you have that "the sky is green" feeling? That's what you're reaching for! You'll say, "I know for a fact that I have enough confidence in me that this is the right action to take. I'm standing in a place that from my perspective I can see the path and I know that it works and I'm taking it." You'll stand in your own authentic power.

Business Ownership Mindset

3. **Self-Doubt**

It's got to be gone. Especially as an entrepreneur and a business owner, you're breaking into new ground. You're in charge of that. Everyone is going to be looking to you and you have to be that rock.

When someone is afraid to make any decisions for fear of being wrong and they back into a corner and never take a stand, they say, "I don't know, but I think maybe it's this way. Oh no. It wasn't. I was wrong."

They flip flop. At some point you want to stop and ask why you think you're wrong. Is it because you don't listen to people? Is it because you listen to too many people? Is it because you didn't trust yourself? If you're going to let self-doubt run your life then self-doubt is the CEO of your company and not you. It's obvious that can't be in a growth position.

It's ok to be wrong, it's ok to not know, and it's ok to be a lot of things as long as you're authentic and you're aware of the choices you're making and you're not just a pinball in a pinball machine going, "I have to do this." And "I have to do that." And I have to do the other thing." It's taking the time to sit down and think, "What do I really want?"

"Where am I at?"

"What do I really want to create?"

"What do I really need to know in order to decide which way I want to go?"

And it's ok that there's this dilemma going on inside of you going, "Which way do I want to go? This is one way we could go and this is the other way we could go. Give me some information and let's make a decision."

Most corporate decision makers will go this direction. That's why

Business Ownership Mindset

they surround themselves with others in consultation. That's why you want strategy meetings, and that's why you want to surround yourself with quality support.

You have to be willing to say, "I believe this. I'm taking a stand and we're going in this direction." That's how you speak from the heart. People will see this and they'll know. They will follow, even if you're wrong once in a while. You'll get better and better at it and that's what builds leaders.

Don't get me wrong it's not like there will come a time when you never doubt yourself... At least I've yet to see anyone get to that point. However, there will be a time with enough practice where you can make a decision quickly, ignore the doubts that might come up and change your mind rarely. That's the ideal as I see it. There will ideally be some flexibility but not due to doubt, it's due to getting new information that comes at a time when it makes sense to change direction.

I get it, that can be a difficult time to identify, and we'll address that in another chapter. In this chapter, I want to you to get the concept that you making a decision, right or wrong and following it through, is a far more powerful position that needing to be right so badly that you can't make a decision at all.

You need to understand that there are really two kinds of failure and one has been mislabeled as failure because it's not failure at all.

Attempting to do something and not having it go the way you planned isn't failure. It's a learning opportunity and I get it sometimes you can have grandiose learning opportunities. The problem with GLO's, as I like to call them because it sounds impressive, is that in the past we've been laughed at, shamed and generally battered for having had them. Paradoxical to the shame, they're actually the most valuable experiences we can have because there's such a vast amount of knowledge that can be gained from them.

Business Ownership Mindset

The other kind of failure is quitting. Don't quit. I have a fitness trainer that is constantly attempting to get me to the point of "failure". She says to me, "keep going until you fail." If I quit while I still have good form, I get "the look", and needless to say, I carry on. That is quitting. However when I do it until that point where I start to lose good form and my muscle is fatigued, not my brain, then I have got to the sweet spot, the good kind of failure. I get to The Peter Principle of fitness training, if you will. ;)

Business Ownership Mindset

4. **Know it all**

Arrogance, on the other hand, comes from someone who thinks they have all the answers and that doesn't work in business either. As soon as you start hiring people you have to be willing to let go of that to some extent, or as a company you're not going to grow. You can survive as a solopreneur that way and you can survive in management that way, but you can't survive business ownership that way. In order to grow as a company owner, you have to become more comfortable in knowing that it's ok to not know.

Some people say, "if I'm going to make a decision and I'm going to go back on my decision because I was wrong, then that's a sign of weakness", and they shy away from it. You can't say that. Well, you can, but that's fear based thinking.

When you stand your ground, you make a decision and then you get more information that shows that you were wrong, feel free to say, "I was wrong!"

There is SO much power in that! You have no doubt in yourself and your abilities to take the proverbial ship and go this way. And, when you see you were wrong to redirect and say, "Its ok. We're going to make it!"

It's important to be able to admit when you're wrong. If you get new information that is contradictory to what you had, admit it and move on.

People who have difficulty in opening up to other possibilities limit themselves and their company's growth. Yes you can go into meetings knowing what you want and brow beat people until they all agree with what you want. Or, you can go in with an open mind, discuss the merits of each alternative, and in the end make a decision. Let people

Business Ownership Mindset

know why you've come to that conclusion and that it includes their input.

Really that's the approach that's needed. Otherwise there's no point in having these people around and they likely won't stay. You can build a bigger business by growing with other's input otherwise you're only growing to the extent of your own wherewithal.

A true thought leader knows that their thoughts haven't been created before, and you can't create from templates of the past, so you have to do creative work. Yes, you'll have a vision and you'll stay steadfast to that vision and yes you may have decided on a path to go there but you'll be in a much more powerful position to take into account feedback when the ships hit shore than to than to adamantly blazon on forward. (Unless you have a plan to give the ship wheels, in which case, you're good to go!)

I know it can seem like a fine line to walk. When you know, and you know you know, you may appear arrogant and that's ok. But when you're when you're looking down at the people in front of you as if they're insignificant idiots, you probably want to sit down and take some personal inventory.

A little introspection goes a long way in building a company. If you have people on your team that aren't in line with your passion then you may want to consider whether they belong in a different position or if they belong on your team at all.

If you're passionate about your goal and people on your team aren't in alignment with you, it doesn't mean that you change direction to match them because that takes away from your message.

What you may have to do is reshuffle them. When you do that from a heart centred place people will respond. They'll either remove themselves on their own accord or they'll step up to the challenge.

What you may have to do is learn better communication skills and

Business Ownership Mindset

become more influential.

What you may have to do is a matter of circumstances. But, when you ask yourself, "Am I ignoring vital information for the protection of my ego?", "Am I taking into account really insightful information that could help me?" or "Is there a better/easier/smarter way to get the result I want?" then you'll find that you can go from know it all to a thought provoking leader.

Listen to your passion, respect your team and you'll go a long way in building your company.

Business Ownership Mindset

Chapter 7
How to Succeed as a Business Owner

1. <u>Know what you want and go after it.</u>

I'm sure you've heard it before, but I'm going to say it again because I don't think anyone can study this fairly short sentence enough.

Our thoughts create our feelings,

Our feelings create our actions, and

Our actions create our results.

In short form we'll write TFA=R

If you think about it, nothing manmade escapes this formula. An architect thinks of a building in her mind, she feels drawn toward the idea knowing that it's a possibility, she begins to take action and formulate a team, and eventually going through this process over and over again, eventually the building is built. I'll grant you it's a simplified version of it, but study it in sincerity and you'll see that everything you create in your life originates in your thoughts, those thoughts become amplified into feelings, you take action towards or away from something and a result is created.

So now, your question should be, "What does this have to do with my business?"

The answer is; everything.

If the results you're creating are the result of the thoughts you think and you don't currently like your results, then you might want to become more intimately involved with your thoughts and beliefs.

And yes, your thoughts in this equation aren't only the thoughts

Business Ownership Mindset

you're thinking today, they're the thoughts you've been thinking since you began thinking. Every decision you've ever made, every assumption you've ever implanted in your brain, they all contribute to the feelings that you have today that move you toward or away from actions, all of which contribute to your results.

I know, this can be a hard one to swallow, let alone digest, but if you allow yourself to study it and see how it truly affects you, then you can see the power of choosing your thoughts to create the results that you want.

This section alone is the basis of a lot of books, but for now we're going to assume that you're on board with the concept and now we're going to see how to turn it into something awesome!

Business Ownership Mindset

2. <u>**Reverse engineer your plan.**</u>

You remember the architect that built the building? We'll I'm guessing that when you read that, in your mind you pictured the completed building even when we were at the "Thought" of the building stage. The reason I guess that is because most of us will think in completed pictures, we only break down the steps when they're required and for the most part will think in completed steps. So like the architect, you're going to build a business, a legacy, or an empire with the end in mind. You're going to start with the biggest boldest picture that you can muster in your mind and then we're going to start reverse engineering the plan. The reason we want to do it this way is because it's actually easier to start with the end in mind and back track to today, than it is to start with today and try to build up the plan. It's not to say that there's a right and wrong way of doing it, it's simply that when you start with the end in mind you have walls set up within your mind, within which you will work. Without those walls, the infinite amount of options can become too much for us to fathom and we run the risk of shutting down. With the walls already in place, it is much easier to lift the roof first, and see the walls. Remove the walls, and see the floor. Remove the floor and see the foundation. Remove the foundation and see the hole that the foundation rests on.

To begin building the building from here looking forward, it seems silly if it occurs to you at all to start by digging a hole. And, without the hole, the foundation breaks.

So, we're going to start with the end in mind, and reverse engineer a plan. A well-engineered plan will be broken down to the point of doable tasks. In other words, you know your plan is solid when the list of action items are broken down to the point that you know how to do them. For example; 'Hire a manager' is not a task, unless you've done it so many times that you already know how to do it. 'Write a job

Business Ownership Mindset

description' may not even be a task unless you've done it so many times that you know how to do it. 'Write a list of all the things I want my manager to do' may indeed be a task, because you do know all of the things that you don't want to do anymore. In short, if you don't know how to do it then keep breaking it down because your brain has a tendency to think in completed pictures and that can be deceiving.

Business Ownership Mindset

3. <u>**Strategize**</u>

      This will become more and more evident, if it isn't already that tremendous amounts of time can be saved by thinking strategically before you think tactically about how you're going to build your business. Just as your thoughts precede your action in the TFA=R formula, your strategic thinking should precede your tactical thinking repeatedly and not just initially. In fact, you're going to want to put some strategic thinking time blocks into your calendar annually, monthly and weekly in order to ensure that you're constantly on track. Just like it doesn't make sense for a pilot flying from LA to Tokyo to only look at the trajectory once in LA and never again, it doesn't make sense for you to put together a business plan once and never strategize about it again until you hopefully land at your destination.

We're going to get into a whole discussion about Strategic Thinking; what it is, why you want it, why you want it so often, how to think strategically and how to flip back to Tactical Thinking. It's paramount to a successful Business. Most entrepreneurs don't understand why they fail at growing into a Business Ownership Mindset and this tends to be the single most reason.

Business Ownership Mindset

4. **Ask for what you want, especially help**

How do people run businesses without knowing how to ask for help? That question, I really don't have an answer for, however I do know that there are A LOT of solopreneurs who are abysmal at asking for what they want and furthermore accepting it once they've asked for it. In the realm of asking for help??? Pshaw. It's even worse.

We can even back up the bus even further, in recognizing that most people don't have a vision or goals established for what they want to create. Without that vision or goals it's nearly impossible to know what the plan is. Without the plan, there's really no way of knowing what the next step is, and without the next step, there's really no way to know what they want. And of course, if you don't know what you want, how can you possibly ask for it???

I know, you're reading this thinking, "I ask for what I want!"

Do you? Do you really?

We used to run a class and in that class people would be set up in groups of 8. Before they got into the groups they would be instructed that they would have 30 seconds to ask the group for something that they wanted. I would then go into 30 minutes of instruction on what to ask for and how to ask for it if they didn't know, but if they did know they could use their 30 seconds any way they wanted to.

In all the years of running that class I might have seen a dozen people who knew how to articulately ask for what they wanted and have it be something useful that got them closer to their goals. It was well under once percent of the population.

And then, to see how the majority reacted when they got what they asked for was nothing short of ludicrous. It became very evident to me why the majority of people fail to grow beyond their current level of

Business Ownership Mindset

success. They're terrified of asking for what they want, and when they get it, they almost surely reject it whether consciously or unconsciously.

In order to truly succeed, you are going to have to prepare your mind that it's ok to ask for what you want. It's ok to learn communication skills that allow you to more eloquently ask for what you want. It's ok to learn communication skills that allow other people to want to deliver on what you ask for. And, it's ok to receive gracefully that which you have asked for! I'm ok if you even accept it sloppily! Just allow yourself to receive! And maybe even keep it! And maybe even take action on creating more!

I don't mean to be facetious at all, (or rude) but when you realize how badly other people want to work with you and give you their gifts and support; you will be blown away by how much you've been turning away all this time.

Business Ownership Mindset

5. What most people think failure is and why it is essential to success.

In the last chapter I touched on the two different types of failure; GLO's and quitting. I'm sure you agree that you're not going to quit so let's look further into Grandiose Learning Opportunities.

Bob Proctor uses a brilliant scale for the 7 Levels of Awareness and it explains how we increase our level of awareness in a given state from not knowing to mastery.

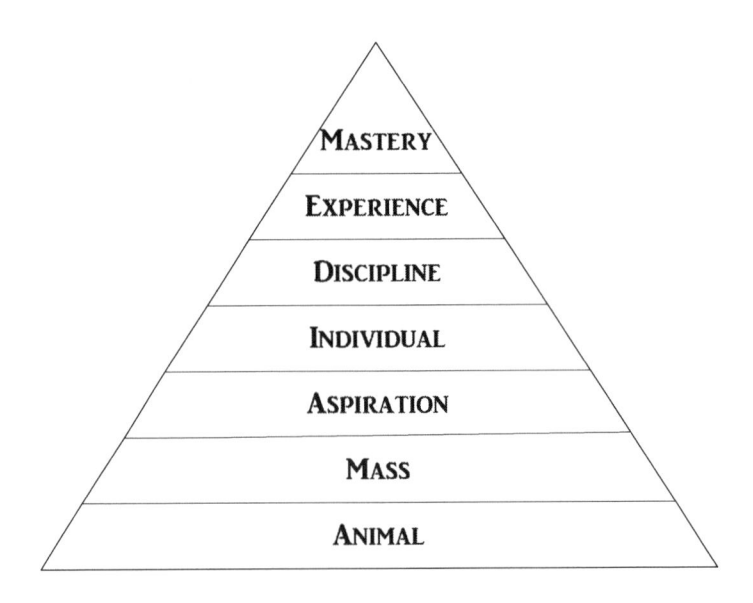

MASTERY
EXPERIENCE
DISCIPLINE
INDIVIDUAL
ASPIRATION
MASS
ANIMAL

In order to achieve mastery we need to pass through the level of Experience. In this stage we practice or play with a concept in order to understand it, in order to comprehend the ins and outs of it. And, in order to understand something we need to be willing to "fail" at it. If we want to master learning to ride a bike, we need to be willing to fall off of it. If we want to be a master architect we need build designs that fail. If

Business Ownership Mindset

we want to master the skill of driving a fork lift we need to learn what makes them tip. It doesn't matter what "it" is that we want to master; we cannot master anything unless we're first willing to go through the stage of experience and that requires our willingness to fail.

There was a great story about a manager who made a colossal error in judgement and it cost the company hundreds of thousands of dollars. Needless to say the manager got invited into the owners office. With his head held low he says, "I know I'm fired. I'll get my things and go."

The owner exclaims, "Fired? Are you kidding me! With this much experience I'm not going to give you to the competition! You're going to make me a fortune!"

Seriously though, you don't need epic failures in order to run an epic company, but if you do find yourself in the midst of an epic failure, simply refer to it as a Grandiose Learning Opportunity and assure yourself that you are on your way to running an epic company.

If you want more information on The 7 Levels of Awareness contact the office and we'll gladly get that to you.

Business Ownership Mindset

Chapter 8
The importance of a vision

1. **Being a Visionary.**

Thought leaders, if you will, build a vision. And they create that vision by looking at themselves, seeing what they bring to the world, how they see the world transforming, and what they want to contribute to that. There's a lot of introspection and not a lot of extrospection. A lot of people, especially smaller entrepreneurs will look at their world and see an accountant and think, "I want to be an accountant." Or, "My boss is making a ton of money. I want to make a ton of money. I'll be the boss." They're always looking externally from themselves for what they want to create. And that doesn't really create a "vision", it starts a company. But to be able to look inside and ask yourself, "What do I really want to create?"

"If I could do it anyway I wanted to."

If you start to extrapolate what's going on inside, and then create this thing called a vision.

What is that 'thing' that's burning inside of you that you don't have a clue how it's going to happen?

And yes, there are the people that have to build on it and it comes a bit at a time. They borrow a goal and they go after it, and from there they start to notice some things that are interesting to them. From there they build on it a little more and little more and hopefully in the end it becomes some 'thing'.

And then there's those who know what it is and just go after it. Some people know at the age of four what they want to be and they go

Business Ownership Mindset

after it in earnest.

The difference is that one group is looking externally for inspiration and the other is looking internally for expression. One says, "I want to be like that." And the other says, "I want to be like me."

Either way can happen consciously and we choose it, or unconsciously and we just go about making it happen. Either way, some people are just good at things and others have to work at it to get there, and that's ok. It just is what it is. For those who don't have a vision though, we're here to help them create it.

Business Ownership Mindset

2. <u>Reverse engineer vs buildout.</u>

Most people, who look to build out their dreams, look out from where they are out toward their dream and ask, "How can I get there?" Whereas I'd like you to shift your thinking around and let's pretend you've already got it, and ask, "How do I get back here?" Start looking back to the present. When we do that in our heads, it actually makes more sense. We can create that vision faster.

Looking from where I'm at to where I want to be, we get stuck in lack and limitation thinking. "I don't have the money", "I don't have the resources", "I don't have the la la la." But when I look at it from the end knowing that I have to get it done in say five years, then I hustle up and think, "Ok I have all this stuff done in 5 years", and I'm assuming it's all done.

It's not asking, "What's the first thing I have to do to get there?" It's calculating back to what the foundational steps were. I'm actually going to start with, "What's the last thing I'll put in place to get it done?"

Of course the idea isn't that you get yourself stuck onto a path. The path will change, but the milestones will likely be the same. And, when you're aiming for the milestone, you know you're on track. With the vision in mind, opportunities will open up that initially, you couldn't even fathom. We've all heard that fact is stranger than fiction and nowhere is that more true than on the path to creating a vision, in my experience.

Business Ownership Mindset

Chapter 9
Creating a Vision

1. **The Process**

   a. **Business Plan**

      i. **Importance of Me.inc**

When we go through the goal planning, you really want to think of your life as me Inc. Think of it as a corporation. And, just like a corporation, you have so much time in a day, you have so many resources, you have so many people around you, and you have whatever else you have. Think of it as having these 6 divisions in your company: They're your health, your social life, your primary relationship, your finances, your personal mastery and your business mastery.

You're in business for yourself so it should be a simple transition to make. The idea that we want you to get out of this is not that you take care of your business and your spouse takes care of everything else. Look at it as this is your entire company and you need all divisions running and functioning happily, in order for the company to function happily. Just like your company can't function with sales rocking it but operations sucks. You can't function with your finances rocking it but your health sucks. It's not going to work. Operations can't rock and have sales suck either. You have to have that balance in business and likewise you have to have that balance in your life. You're going to have to figure out your goals as far as your personal skill sets go outside of your occupation. That could be painting, or motorbike riding, whatever it is, it's the fun stuff that you do.

Once you establish goals in all areas of your life, now the framework is set and all divisions are functional. Now you can go and run your company with fervour because you have a life. You have to have

Business Ownership Mindset

enough time to play.

When you do this, take enough time to work through your discomfort of what's holding you back in other divisions. One aspect you'll want to be asking yourself is how does Me Inc. serve society? Instead of just a division that invests in the community, how does the company serve the community? It's not just that Me Inc is making money hand over fist and donating a token of appreciation to society but what's the real integration?

I know it sounds crazy, but not only in the end will you be more satisfied with what you've accomplished, but the extent of what you can do now will be more...well...extensive!

Your imagination will always grow to fill the space that you allow it. When you open up from "What can I do in this office?" to "What can I do in our community?" or even "How can I serve society?" your brains functions kick into motion and bigger and better ideas start to flow.

Business Ownership Mindset

ii.   20, 10, 5, and 1 year goals

When people have a vision that is in line with their passion and it's in service to society people are all over it! The CEO has to pull them back and remind them to go home at the end of the day. So how do you create that in your company, you ask? The answer is simple; you create it in your mind first.

It's a strange phenomenon to me that most people's income is in direct correlation to the span of their goals. What do I mean by that? Well if you look at most people earning a base wage their goals are usually out about a week. The big highlight of their life is Friday, or whatever day of the week their weekend begins. When people start to stretch and have one year goals, their income increases substantially. When people stretch even more and have 5 year goals, their income increases substantially yet again, and likewise with 10 and 20 year goals. I say most people, because some people are transitioning. They may have 5 year goals, but they are in the process of building them.

I don't write this to get your judgemental genes flared. I write this to inspire you to set more long term goals. And no I don't mean plan on having a beer 20 years from now. I mean set goals that starting today are going to take you 20 years to achieve.

If you need some inspiration in this domain Peter Diamandis and Elon Musk are two of the most openly sharing visionaries for not only demonstrating their abilities but also for sharing how they think.

Now I'm no Diamandis or Musk, and I don't think you need to be either. What I do think though, is that having immense goals that may take decades or even life times to accomplish achieves a multitude of functions beyond the accomplishment of the goal itself. Having a 20 year goal pushes your brain to function and to think in ways that 10 or 5 year goals cannot push your brain. It forces your creativity and ingenuity. It

Business Ownership Mindset

forces your focus and your will. It forces your perspective and it forces your reason. It forces all of those beyond what it would with shorter term goals. Of course if you've only been thinking one year ahead, then starting to think 5 years out will force your thinking more than you have up until now. Likewise from 5 to 10. So wherever your mind is now, stretch it beyond that!

So now you get to go do it! Now, Go Do It! NGDI or as we like to call it GSD. (For the purpose of maintaining our General Audience rating on this book, if you can't figure out what GSD is, then simply stick with NGDI as your moto)

1. Write a list of all the things you want to accomplish in your life. Include everything that is silly, unrealistic and …just because.
2. Categorize them into Business, Social and Personal. Take the Business and separate them into
    a. Business Mastery and
    b. Financial

    Take the Social and separate them into

    c. Friends
    d. Family and
    e. Intimate Relationship
         (If you have or want one)

    Take the Personal and separate them into

    f. Personal Mastery and
    g. Health

    If there's a category that's light on goals write some more. You should have a healthy balance in all areas. Remember Me inc?

3. Once you have a solid fix on all areas of your life, put a date of accomplishment on them. It might be an exact date that you want to achieve things but it might just be the year a year from

Business Ownership Mindset

now, five years from now, 10 years from now or even 20 years from now. And, appreciate that some of those goals are going to be tasks set 20 years in the future, such as go for a bike tour in Holland on my 100th birthday.

4. Now identify your 1 year, 5 year, 10 and 20 year goals. The goals that will actually take that long to accomplish from start to accomplishment.

    If you don't have any in a given category, encourage yourself to set some. Yes, even if it feels silly or contrived. Evoke your imagination and ask, what if I did have a 20 year goal?

Business Ownership Mindset

iii.   Legacy

Sadly enough when I look up legacy the definition comes up as an amount of money or property left to someone in a will. That is an inheritance not a legacy. A legacy is the impact that someone leaves after their gone. You may have already left a few legacies; at school or previous companies. You may have had a band, or even left a legacy in sports. You don't have to be dead to leave a legacy; you just have to have made an impact. And no, it doesn't take 20 years to build a legacy. It can happen in 5 years or even one. They can be good or bad. They can be motivating or ominous and warning. They can be self-perpetuating and eternal. There are a lot of things that legacies can be and there are a lot of benefits that building a legacy can achieve.

Building your legacy can not only provide people with resources after you're gone, but they can also benefit you while you're building it. As with long term goals, building a legacy will help you to expand the capacity of your mindset and awareness. It can also help to increase your brain function. It can also help to create feelings of purpose, fulfillment, gratitude and generosity.

In Man's Search for Meaning, Victor Frankle points out that any pursuit that a person has can give them drive, purpose and meaning if they give that pursuit enough meaning. When you identify the legacy that you would like to leave on this planet, the legacy that you would like your company to leave on the world and the legacy that you would like to leave your company with, you will have a pursuit with a substantial amount of meaning; enough to give your every breath meaning, enough to give your every morning meaning, and, enough to give your life meaning. So much so that no one will be able to argue it.

In an ideal world your company will leave a legacy no matter what. But sadly some are quickly forgotten. The only way to ensure that

Business Ownership Mindset

your company leaves a legacy is to consciously and intentionally build it.

The question I have for you now is, "What kind of legacy do you want to leave?"

Business Ownership Mindset

b. What problem do you solve for your client?

This is where your service to society integrates into your vision. It's not just that people need a 'pen'. Of course, Yes you want to figure out what problem you solve for your client, but you also want to figure out how you can provide for something that is of benefit to your client, and also how you can make the world a better place for their contacts because of the solution you provide to your client. It's not just selling someone a pen, it's questioning what are they going to do with the pen and what are they creating? How do we create a manifesto that goes beyond a single point? It's not just how do we create the best pen for our client to sign contracts, but how do we create a pen for our client that inspires them to write, better contracts…or something to that effect.

What problem you solve for your client might be considered a 1 - 5 year outlook. That's very important to have because you have a market place that is moving a certain direction.

Another question you'll want to ask is, what problems will my clients face in the future that they're not aware of today? And, that is your 10 – 20 year outlook. And, how do they line up such that if I solve their problem today, that it lines up with my 20 year vision of what problems will they come across or avert so they won't even know that they've averted the problem because they couldn't even see it. And, that's where the vision takes place. (Maybe it's inventing ink that doesn't dry, because 20 years from now maybe no one is using pens and if they find yours, they'll still be able to use it.) ((Yes, that's sarcasm. Have a little fun with it.))

Another way to ask it is, "How do I serve society today?" and "How do I serve society in the long run?", "What if there was a way to help society be more resilient? And, what might that look like in a way that I can contribute with my passion and my talents?"

Business Ownership Mindset

When you start to ask the questions, you can start to find ways to slot yourself in, in however of a small way that you want.

It's not unheard of to have something like a pen company donate a wing to a hospital, or maybe even a school. When you're not focused on selling a pen but rather selling a vision the pen becomes the means to the end. It's a vehicle to get you there.

It's a simple distinction of how you want to serve society today and how you want to serve them in the future.

In case you're not seeing it yet, the reason for this long- term global-impact type thinking isn't simply to be a compassionate capitalist although it may help with that. The reason you want to start thinking this way is so that your company becomes larger than just you and where you're at today. It's so that your daily decisions have a predetermined destination. It's so that you become a Business Owner.

Business Ownership Mindset

c. **Where do you fit in the market?**

This can be a dangerous question to ask because you may fall into a hole that you don't want to be in. You may want to start by asking where do I want to be in the market? Then ask where you fit in the market? And if there's a gap between the two then you can decide how to get from where you are to where you want to be. Knowing where you fit in the market, though, can have a tremendous impact on how you market and sell yourself. If we go back to the pen example, maybe right now you look at the market and think it's delivery is through office supply stores. But what if you want to be a high end signature pen? Then maybe that positioning would be more suited to high end men's wear or bridal stores.

You may already be well established in a market, but if that market doesn't suit where you want to be then you're going to have to seriously sit down and strategize on where you want to be and how you're going to get there. One consideration is going to have to be on revenue replacement moving into the new market. If you're not an established name in the new market, you're going to at least have an idea of how long it's going to take to get established and whether or not there's a transition plan or just a jump and go plan. The biggest mistake I see people make is deciding on where they fit into the market before they've established their long-term goals and legacy. If you're just starting and wanting to make a name for yourself, make sure you know where you want to be long-term because a lot of money and effort is going to go into getting you established.

If, on the other hand, you find yourself in the wrong market due to a change in plans or market place then, yes, you're going to have to decide when and how to cut your losses and get positioned in the right market. Sometimes this can seem as simple as a business coach who has been working with corporations who decides that they would be better

Business Ownership Mindset

positioned with entrepreneurs. That may seem like a simple transition, but it's not. The language those two groups speak is completely different. Their mindsets are completely different! It would be easier to transition from a male focused clientele to a female focused clientele, and obviously that would be a huge change. At least in the later example not all of the material would have to change, it could, in theory, just be a branding transition.

If, based on long term goals, the objective is to transition from an in house training model to an online training model it's important to know that those are two completely different markets with a completely different buying style, support systems and technical issues. It's not to say that one doesn't lend itself to the other, but changing your market mid stride is not something to be taken lightly. You'll want to know your long-term goals, your legacy, and your strategy to decide on where you want to fit in the market and how you're going to fit in there.

You want to decide how you're going to bring your company to the market because it'll have a huge influence on the amount of time you spend at work, where you work and how you work. You want to define all of these things before you pick your ideal client so that you're the one deciding these things and not your clients deciding for you.

Business Ownership Mindset

d. Who is your ideal client?

Some people call this your niche but I don't work with a niche, I work with my ideal clients. I know you're my ideal client because you've read this far in the book! The whole time I've been writing, I've been writing to you! Everyone who wasn't my ideal client likely didn't make it past the first chapter! Ok, let's be honest you didn't really read the whole book from the beginning until now. You probably just flipped to this part and started reading here. I know because most of my clients are ADD and wouldn't read a book from beginning to end unless they knew the author and had a meeting tomorrow to talk about the book. Na. Even then they'd flip through it to get the gist of it. ;) Did I mention that my ideal client has a sense of humour?

Without knowing who you REALLY want to work with you'll likely get stuck trying to please everyone and not only does it not please everyone, it'll drive you nuts.

Even if you start with a list of people you don't want to work with, you'll at least be further ahead than trying to work with everyone. Even the pen sales person needs to know who they're not selling too, especially if it's a high end pen!

The piece of this I think most people have an issue with is that they're afraid of being honest with themselves about who they are and what they like. They use the excuse that it's just a product and it's just a market to sell to. That's not true. Even Coke Cola had to decide who their market was. And, everyone who wants to make a career out of working there has to decide that Coke's ideal market is who they want to deal with all day long because if it isn't they're going to end up hating their job in very short order.

As a business owner you don't have to let the market decide who buys your product most often. You get to decide who you want to sell it

Business Ownership Mindset

to. Are there going to be exceptions to that? Of course! Is it possible that your product takes on a life of its own and a totally different market starts to buy your product? Of course! And, when that happens, don't stop people from buying your product. That's just silly. But, until that happens don't just decide who's most likely to buy your product, identify who you want your client to be ideally.

Business Ownership Mindset

e. What is your brand/reputation?

Branding is more than just picking out a logo. It's a representation of how you want people to feel when they interact with you. Branding experts and art therapists understand the significance of colours and shapes have on people. They evoke feelings. It's important to ask yourself, how do I want people to feel? How do I want people to see me and my products? What you really want to ask yourself is, "Am I being my authentic self?" When you are your authentic self and talking about your passion, you will naturally draw people in. You need to know that you're naturally a sales person when you start talking about your passion because you naturally draw people in.

I know it may sound crazy to have such concerns if you're selling a widget. But it really does matter. If you're attempting to market something that's savvy to a posh market when you're true nature is edgy and raw, it could be a tough go. Likewise if you're savvy and posh selling to an edgy and raw market. I'm not saying it can't be done, but it would be a lot easier to stick to your market. Authenticity has a way of attracting the right people faster.

Now you might be questioning the whole fake it 'till you make it concept, but don't. It works and it works great. But the reason it works it because there's a part of you that wants to be developed, nurtured and polished into the new role. If there's an internal draw towards a new way of being then that is authentic! There's a seed inside of you that wants to grow. That's completely different than trying to be something you think you "should" be.

Business Ownership Mindset

f. What projects do you want to take on?

Now that you have all that figured out, your goals, legacy, clients, and branding, you can start to figure out what projects you want to work on. In theory, it should be a lot easier as you know who you're looking for, where to find them and what you want to say to them. Of course you still want to be thinking strategically about the projects that you take on; that they'll be getting you where you want to go, creating the revenue that you want to create and that you're spending your time the way you want to spend your time. Yes, even with all of things in place that we've worked through I have seen people spending time doing things they think they should be doing instead of doing the things they want to be doing that creates revenue. And, I've had people create their business the way they want to and reach the point where it's time to do the things they've set out to do and realize that they're terrified of doing that exact thing. Which, by the way, there is absolutely nothing wrong with. Remember at the beginning of the book when I said that business is the best personal growth program out there? Well, this is exactly where that happens. It happens in doing the things that scare you, that stall you, that take your breath away. It's in doing the things that intimidate you and make you question your intelligence and your competence. It's in all of those things. The freedom you seek is just beyond your comfort zone, so it's not going to be comfortable getting there. No one ever said it would be easy to learn how to ride a bike and no one who's ever run a business will tell you that it's easy either. But, it most certainly is worth it.

Business Ownership Mindset

2. Reverse Engineering it.

   a. Starting with the end goal in mind

   Whether it's the 20 year goal or the one year goals, we're going to look at chunking down the goal into, let's call them bite sized pieces. In every goal there are a multitude of aspects to them. Whether you mind map it or outline your goal, there are going to be major aspects and minor aspects. At this point it's not so important to know which aspects work together, so much as it is to know what the aspects are. For example if you were to build a house, you can break it down into a foundation, walls and a roof, or you could break it down into rooms. At this point, it doesn't really matter how you break it down. What you need to know first, second and third will become evident in a bit.

   Breaking down a business plan into its components works the same way. If you want to become a national franchise you might look at which roles head office is going to take and which roles the satellite offices are going to take. You might look at where you want head office and where you want your satellite offices to be. Either way, you're eventually going to have to figure out both, but how you break it down at this point is irrelevant, you just need to break it down so that you have manageable chunks to work with. From there you're going to identify the major tasks that need to be addressed and then you're going to prioritize them. Obviously, foundations need to be laid before the walls go up, but there's a lot that needs to happen before the foundation can be laid too.

   Start with one of your most important goals to you and then reverse engineer the next most important. You'll likely only want to work on two or three goals at a time, one from Business, one Personal or one from Social. Don't take on too much at once

Business Ownership Mindset

b. What people do you need on your team and when?

   i.   Culture (Accountability/Attitude)

Once you have your major tasks established and they're in chronological order, you're going to want to identify who you want to bring on to help. Of course you're going to want to identify the skills needed to accomplish the tasks, but now is the time that you'll also want to identify your company culture. Knowing who someone is and what they bring to the table besides their acumen is important. Remember that there is a philosophy that you're going to want to maintain. You're going to have to ask if they are they willing to shape it and if not what becomes a deal breaker. You'll want to know that your support is happy with where they're at and are they following their passion too. Hiring someone just because they're good at it won't be enough to create loyalty or sustainability. You want to think about finding people who actually love doing it. And, yes there are people who love doing every job you can think of. It's a fact that it costs 3 times a person's annual salary to invest in them and if they aren't fully productive then you're not going to get that payback. Once they're fully engaged in the job, you want to keep them! Now that you've groomed them, that's when the payoff really begins. It all cycles into "What's the cost of firing someone or having them quit?" You can't just pick somebody because they're good at their job. You have to take into account whether or not their values fit in with the group. Some people think their personality needs to fit in with the group and that's not true. Ideally you want a multitude of personalities in your office. Some will be good with details, some will be good with creativity, some connecting with prospects and some on setting up systems. More often than not those four jobs involve four different people. Especially if their passion lies in that particular area. You can have four very different personality types with the same values. It's those values that you want to be clear on so that you're creating a culture that adheres together.

Business Ownership Mindset

c. **What systems do you need/when?**

You might be wondering at this point, what do systems have to do with mindset? And that is a valid question. It actually has a lot to do with it. In fact any good sales person that sells systems will want to deal directly with the owner not only from a decision making point of view but from a mindset perspective too. Making sure that the systems you choose work with the corporate objectives and culture is paramount to their successful integration. Your systems will enforce your culture.

The first part of that, especially with small business, you want to take the processes out of the owners head and into the hands of your employees. That is the culture, the environment and how the company runs. Of course, in order to have a sellable business you'll need to have the right systems in place to replace you so that the business doesn't need you to maintain not only the revenue, but the culture and environment too.

How you do that? You need to start looking at what you want to systemize; marketing, sales, internal communication, or accounting. You're going to need all of those things systemized and more. Or you might have one system that integrates all of those things.

The biggest mistake I hear from executives is, "I need to do that."

No you don't. Get that out of your head. In an ideal world the only thing you need to do is decide what time you're going to the beach. If you can't systemize and delegate every single thing you do in your company then it's not sellable. And, yes I get that you might not want to sell your business, but it's not a business if it's not sellable. That doesn't mean you have to sell it. And, it doesn't mean that you have to delegate 100% of the tasks. It simply means that you have the mindset to set it up that way, that you could sell it if you wanted to. When you have that mindset you're going to put in better systems to suit your company.

Business Ownership Mindset

i. Work Environment (Resources/Health)

After establishing the kind of culture you want to create, now you're going to identify the work environment. I appreciate that you might already have a work place established. If it's working, great! Keep it! But if it's not working or if you want to improve on it, then you'll want to look at not only what you want to create for yourself and your staff but also the clients experience of your work environment. And that can be the physical space including the lighting, the colours, and the style of furniture. It can also be what the clients hears, the volume of background noise, what people say to clients and what conversations are had or not had, in front of clients and between workers.

You may think that it doesn't matter. Say, if you were in an industrial shop and the clients never go into the shop. But, it does matter what kind of conversations are going on. Is it the kind of shop that people talk about their personal life while they're waiting on machinery or is it the kind of place where no one talks to each other while they're working. It takes two very different kinds of people to work in those two examples. The clearer you are on the kind of environment you want to have, the easier it's going to be to find the right people to work together, who love their jobs and put 100% into their productivity.

Business Ownership Mindset

d. How do you want to get it to market/marketing?

This question can be great fun. Depending on what kind of lifestyle you want, you could get your product out to market any way you want! Especially in today's world, the world's your oyster. You can do bricks and mortar type retail, you can go through distributors, you can set up a multilevel marketing system, you can set up licencing or franchise rights, you can sell it online or you can sell door to door. You could sell it from stage or you can stay at home. Are you getting the idea, because I can keep going?

There is no right or wrong way to get a product to market. The only question you have to answer is how do you want to get it to market? This is the time that you want to take your personality into account. Do you want to be face to face with people or do you want to be sequestered? Do you want to have a lot of people around you or do you want your team to work on their own and only contact you on a need to know basis.

Figuring out where your market is and how to access them will be the next set of questions. You might have to morph some of your marketing channels to accommodate your clientele, but for the most part that just keeps things interesting.

If you don't know where they are or how to get a hold of them, there is plenty of access to that kind of information now on the internet. If you don't know how to access it, borrow a teenager and for some pizza they'll be able to get you what used to cost thousands. Remember: Google is your friend.

Business Ownership Mindset

3. **Strategy for implementation.**

The question you want to ask yourself here is, "Is the business efficient? Do I have the right people and systems doing the right things?"

I have found over the years that most small business owners don't stop and strategize within their business. They simply run after the next thing that they see that needs to get done and they not only feel like the cartoon character trying to stick a finger or toe in every hole in the dam to hold it back from exploding, but some of them even look like that!

In order to stop this chaotic thinking you need to slow down and give yourself some time to think. Start asking yourself the right questions.

Questions like;

Now that I have a vision how many ways could I solve this problem?

Have I solved this problem in the past?

If so, what worked then?

Could I use that system again or do I need a new system?

If I need a new system, what does the new system need to include?

Sometimes people will implement a new system, like a software package and they don't stop to assess whether or not the company is being diverted down the wrong path due to limitations of the system rather than identifying if they're still on track to achieve their vision. They'll actually get their entire team to organize around the structure and they don't look at the software and ask which is better to maintain the software and the direction we're going, or to change the software and get back on track for the direction the owner believes they should be going. It again requires asking questions.

Business Ownership Mindset

Questions like;

> Why are we doing this?
>
> Is this getting us toward our long term goals too?
>
> What should we be doing more of?
>
> What should we be doing less of?

An example of this is when I had an executive who asked, "I want you to look at everything you do, and ask 'Why are you doing this?'" And the guys in the field looked at it from a narrow perspective and asked, "Why are we sending all of this outage data to head office?" and they didn't see any value in it. They just saw it as extra work. So they decided not to send any of the outage data statistics to HO. Meanwhile the guys in the engineering office would never talk to the field guys, give feedback or let them know what they were discovering with the outage data. They were however relaying that information to the electrical association to show how the grid was performing. Then the electrical association would compare the grid to other grids across North America and they would give back statistical analysis of the performance compared to the other grids. Something to the effect of, here's the industry average and this grid is either higher or lower than that average. Well, guess what? This grid for the five years that they didn't submit the data was performing amazingly well! Of course it did, because there was no outage data being captured or submitted. Now ironically they think they're just rocking it! They're the cream of the crop! Of course the retail sector started branding it that they had the most reliable system in the network. Unfortunately, it was all false. Not out of malice or mockery but simply because they quit taking data in the field because someone asked what expenses could be cut without looking at the bigger picture of how that activity interacted with the overall goal.

Personally I thought the whole thing was hilarious, no harm no foul, but you really do have to understand how important a strategic way

Business Ownership Mindset

of looking at the business is and that it's far more important than simply cutting expenses or going after the a new market trend.

Business Ownership Mindset

4. <u>Overcoming Obstacles.</u>

Overcoming obstacles can be an ongoing occurrence for anyone, but for the Business Owner, it's a way of life. Get used to it. Better yet, get good and it and enjoy it. Practice becoming a problem solving machine. Or better yet, don't refer to them as problems, refer to them as challenges. Think of them as a puzzle that you get to solve. If you already refer to them as challenges start referring to them as opportunities. There is a law of nature called the law of dichotomy that says that everything has an equal and opposite aspect to it. There is a "good" and "bad" to everything; for every up there's a down, for every right there's a left. Therefore, for every problem there's an opportunity. As I drink my tea, there's a problem; I'm running out of tea. But there's also an opportunity; I have room in my cup for something else. Train yourself that for every problem there's an opportunity. The easiest way to do that is to simply call the situation an opportunity.

Know that your brain is a problem solving machine. Whatever you throw at it, it has to make sense of it. So if you tell yourself that a situation is an opportunity, it will find the opportunity because it has to make sense of it. The more you do that, the more easily you'll find the opportunities.

If you're already in the habit of calling them opportunities then start referring to them as gifts. For every problem is indeed a gift from the universe to help you to become smarter, better, more experienced and it builds character.

I know people who can't handle getting a hang nail. Their life gets derailed, plans get cancelled and their entire mental capacity is lodged into the catastrophe of nail hygiene. No, I'm not kidding. And, yes they are sane and functional. But no, they are not Business Owners. They can't be. Not only does being a Business Owner require a vision, it also requires

Business Ownership Mindset

the ability to see things for what they are not for the calamity that they could be. It reminds me of the person who yells, "You almost hit that!" as if it's the worst thing that could ever happen. You're mindset needs to be, "but, I didn't hit it. So it's all good."

A friend of mine once said, "You're not really in business until you get sued." Ya, that's kind of sad, but it's also kind of true. No, I don't think you need to get sued to be in business. But you do need to get to the point where even going to court is just a part of your day. You just deal with it in a pragmatic, practical way. It might be over something you did or it might just be for land distribution or who knows what. But getting emotionally derailed just because something is going on in your life isn't going to help you.

So you may be asking how you're supposed to do this; how do you calm your mind in the midst of chaos? There are numerous ways! It's no different than letting go of your resistance that we talked about in the beginning of this book. Simply replace the word problem with challenge, opportunity or gift. You can also do meditation, Success Therapy, deep breathing exercises, reading books on 'the' subject so that you become more familiar with it, and just knowing that you don't need to freak out at freaky circumstances can be enough too! Practice will be your best friend.

You're going to get so good at overcoming obstacles that one day, what seems like a calamity today, will be a moot point to you then.

Business Ownership Mindset

5. Leadership Mindset

This could be a whole book unto itself. It may well be as you're reading this. If you like this book, you're going to love my book on leadership. ;)

Rule number one to leadership, if no one is following then you're not really leading. I know that you could run your company like a dictator. Many people have and many of their companies could be considered successful. However, the price these people pay for that choice is not a price I want to pay and it's not a price most people I know want to pay. The good news is there's another choice and it's called leadership. By leading people to become successful, you not only feel better about yourself, you surround yourself with better people. Not to say that dictators don't have good people working for them, because they can. But, the amount of people you don't want to surround yourself with is substantially higher. Leaders act like a beacon and they attract to them a certain kind of person and they repel the opposite kind of person. And, that's ok! In fact, it's great! For all the people that you repel, someone else will attract. Don't worry. They'll be taken care of.

So what makes a leader a good leader? Surprisingly amiability is not essential. You can't be a complete jerk, but you don't have to be "nice" to everyone. Sometimes the need to be nice is actually a deterrent to leadership.

We covered some of the traits like being a visionary and having a practical approach to chaos or crisis. But having a vision isn't enough, you also have to be able to communicate that vision and inspire others to take action. One of the easiest ways to do that will be through living your passion, because when we live our passion we naturally inspire others. When we live in our passion we also tend to be more creative which helps to problem solve and to communicate more effectively. One thing that a

Business Ownership Mindset

leader needs to be is an effective interpreter. Even though some leaders lead through fear, they're still inarguably effective communicators in interpreting the importance of a situation to their followers. That's not a strategy I recommend, leading by fear is toxic on the mind and body. And, in a company, you want to encourage a growth mentality. Growth of the company and of its people. In a growth and success oriented atmosphere people will grow and succeed, which means your company will too! By facilitating a growth atmosphere in your company you'll also better your followers' ability to judge risk and to take action. Both of which are extremely important leadership skills. A true leader nurtures an atmosphere of leadership. Set your people up for success and teach them how to lead and you will create a company that becomes self-perpetuating legacy.

Business Ownership Mindset

Chapter 10
The importance of honouring your Choices

1. **It's the only way to get things done.**

If you don't, no one else will.

You've created a vision and you've reverse engineered it, now it's time for the rubber to Hit the road and actually do it. Unfortunately, a lot of people get this far, but then they don't honour their choices.

They have a goal, they have a plan to get there, they announce, "I think we should do this!" and someone steps in and says, "No actually, we have to do this other thing."

And, off they go doing that other thing. The other person somehow is automatically right for whatever reason. Maybe it's because they have credentials so they're perceived as smarter, or they are the one that deals with the issue, so their immediate knowledge of the situation dictates that this other thing has precedence or maybe it's the client and they have the pay cheque. For whatever reason, they're not honouring their own choices. For some reason they're giving their power up to these other people.

At no point are they saying to themselves, "Hey! I've made this plan. I know what this plan looks like and this is the way it's going down. I appreciate that this person is an engineer or that person is smarter than me, but what if we did it this way and what might it look like?" or, "I've set this time to start working on it right now. I'm going to work on this right now and we can meet in half an hour and then I'll listen to whatever is going on for you."

Business Ownership Mindset

Now, it could be confusing that I'm contradicting what I said earlier about diversity and taking other people's opinions into account, but I'm not.

I'm talking about once you've made a decision then you have to stick with it and see it to fruition. The question here is how do you do that when the old questions, and the old way of doing things get in the way?

Business Ownership Mindset

2. <u>Your logical mind knows the plan.</u>

When it comes down to doing something and actually implementing it, this is where people's mindset gets in the way of moving forward on the plan. This goes beyond setting up the Gant charts and projection sheets. What we're really talking about here is setting up your week and setting up your month so that your logical mind can make the best decisions possible for you, so that when it comes time to doing something, your emotional mind doesn't take you out of the game.

The question is, "How do you lay it out so that it makes the most amount of sense?"

You may be thinking, "At this point in time, I've said that 'this' is the best time for me to...(whatever)...start writing the book."

And all of a sudden, somebody calls in and says, "Oh I really need your help right now!"

You have to be able to say something to the effect of, "You know, right now won't work. I will help you in half an hour though."

And in your mind be thinking, "I'm sticking to my plan. I'm going to get this done. I said now was the best time, so I'm doing it now."

Yes, this refers back to the chapter on how to fail in business and thinking that other people's needs are more important.

From a time blocking perspective this is all really kind of basic, however time blocking is repeatedly one of most people's biggest issues. They don't honour their own time and do the things they said they were going to do, when they said they were going to do them. So the plans keep getting laid away depending on someone else's alligators and fires.

You have to be able to declare, "I said I was going to do this, at this time, so I'm going to do it!"

Business Ownership Mindset

And, be able to gently push someone aside and go, "I'll get to you in a minute."

It's paramount.

The question from the audience is, "Does honouring your time mean that your time is desirable? It means not yielding to someone else's desires unless it's important to you?"

My answer to that is, "Not necessarily."

And the challenge is this. You may think that solving someone else's alligators is important to you because there's money on the line if you don't deal with it. You may think that this client will fire you if you're not available at their beckon call, but you can't think that way, depending on your agreement of course, if you get paid twice as much to have immediate response time, well then we need to address that. But you have to know that keeping your business alive is more important than solving your clients' problems. If you're not out doing Revenue Generating Activity then it doesn't matter how big of a problem they have. You're going to end up running yourself out of business and they're not going to have you to go to at all the time to solve their problems!

Now you may be thinking, this only happens in a solopreneur situation, but it doesn't. I've seen it happen at almost all levels where people will put their clients or their subordinates problems ahead of their own scheduling and they will repeatedly never get their own work done because they misappropriate their priorities, don't honour their own time management and in the end lose out because they haven't got done the things that they needed to get done in order for their company to move forward.

The issue is this; they logically set a plan, but when it then comes time to go and do it, all of a sudden the fear comes up. Then because there's an emotional charge, it overrules logic and moves them into doing something else. Depending on the fear, they may just want to avoid the

Business Ownership Mindset

work they have planned and decide it's more important to go and scrub the baseboards, with a toothbrush, that they can't find right now, so the go to the store to buy one...

It's the emotions that take them out of the plan. If you have a habit of being available to everyone else's whim, in order to stay on task and keep your priorities your priorities, you have to start honouring your time.

Make a decision to time block; set aside a time when there's no stress in the week to logically look at your week and figure out what makes the most amount of sense. Ask yourself what you need to have in place, what you don't need to have in place and make time for the alligators and fires. You want to have time for those too and that's cool!

Your planning time may be Sunday afternoon, Friday afternoon or whatever works for you. Look at your week when it's not emotional, you can look at your week logically, and you know that your planned schedule will work at least on some level.

Now go and apply it. If you just panicked, don't. There will be a lot more on the actual 'how to apply this' in the next chapter.

What usually happens after this though is that most people will set it up but then completely bypass the schedule. They know they had a plan, but something came up. They say things like, "Oh I was going to meet with kitchen staff today, but something came up." Or "I was going to go check on the show homes but I didn't have time to do it, a deadline came up early on these documents and I had to get them done today."

As you will often hear me say; once is an accident, twice is a mistake but three times and it's a habit. So if it's happened three times, we have to look at that habit and ask, "Why am I not honouring my time?", "Why do I think those things are more important?" and this is when we need to go through a process of introspection and find the answers to these questions. In my opinion Success Therapy is the best

Business Ownership Mindset

way to uncover this because it doesn't just identify the cause of the problem, it resolves the issue.

Another question begs attention from the audience, "But, how do you allow for the spontaneous acts or the internal knowing that you need to act on something that's outside of your plan? I find people often get too caught up with the plan and they don't stop and listen to their bodies to keep them on track. When they listen to their head too much, they fail."

Once you actually know how to honour your time, and say you've stuck to your new habit for three weeks or more, and then some random act occurs like some crazy woman comes into your office but you're fascinated by her and you decide to drop your 12 o'clock commitment and you're going to go out for lunch with her instead. This isn't a habit, it doesn't happen regularly, it just happened this once and you thought, "You know what? I'm going to go with it."

And that's when you know you're going with your heart and allowing the random awesomeness of life to play a role in the success of your plans. It's when it's not a habit and you allow yourself to go off path because it feels good. You especially know if, while doing that spontaneous thing, something happened to move you forward in your goals that wouldn't have happened any other way.

I'll warn you though, if over the past six months you've not done a certain task because something else felt better, then you're kidding yourself. That is a habit and you're avoiding doing the thing and you're using the excuse that something else just felt better.

You have to get in the habit first, knowing that you honour your time, and then when those little idioms happen then they're ok. And then, when there's a car collision in front of you and you were late for the meeting, we can go, "Ya I get it, stuff happens. No big deal. Let's carry on." It's an exception. It's not the rule.

Business Ownership Mindset

3. <u>Your emotional spontaneous mind and sabotage</u>

If it isn't clear by now what the difference is between the woman coming into your office and deciding to go to lunch with her because you found her fascinating and deciding to go for lunch with her because you were avoiding doing that thing that you had planned, one can be defined as emotional spontaneity and the other as avoidance or even self-sabotage.

It really is important to be able to differentiate between the two, because to the unknowing mind the two can look identical. "Someone came into my office and asked me to go to lunch! What? I went. That's what I do."

Yes, it is. And, you don't do what you say you're going to do, and you get frustrated at the end of every week because you don't feel like you're getting ahead, and your business isn't growing the way it should or the way you want it to. If this sounds all too familiar, differentiate between spontaneity and self-sabotage. (Hint: go to the chapters on letting go of resistance.)

Business Ownership Mindset

Chapter 11
How to Honour Your Choices

1. Time Blocking

I really want you to understand that this isn't about pigeonholing you into a decision whether it's a good idea or not. Obviously if new information comes to light then you want to take that information into consideration. However you can't put off making a decision until you have all the information because there's always going to be more information coming! You can go back and reassess the basis of that decision and that's ok (occasionally, or sometimes). But make a decision and stick with it. If in the event that new information comes up that contradicts the basis of that decision then you're obviously free to look at that. (Occasionally, or sometimes)

For years you might not believe in Santa Clause but then all of a sudden there's a big jolly guy coming down your chimney, then all of a sudden you find yourself reassessing that decision. Or if aliens land on your front yard then great! That might be a good time to reassess your decision. It's, you know, a new piece of information worth taking into account. But it's a monumental piece of information that shakes the foundation of your previous decision. Don't let just any piece of information take you astray.

Business Ownership Mindset

2. <u>Micro Time Blocking</u>

This is a fascinating concept, whereby every minute of your day is allocated, including bathroom breaks and teeth brushing. For the purpose of discovering your own resistance towards Time Blocking, it's a great experiment. If you could do this for 30 days, there is no doubt in my mind that you will learn to honour your choices. But, remember once the resistance to Time Blocking is gone, allow for deviations in the plan. Sometimes the universe really does know best. Find the flow.

Business Ownership Mindset

3. <u>**Beliefs Around Time Blocking - how to engage your whole body.**</u>

Let's say that you've given this whole idea a noble attempt for 30 days or so and you're starting to get frustrated with your continual derailment. Relax, you're in good company with about 90% of your class. Here's a little exercise to do, to help you figure out why you keep going back to the old habit.

When it's time to go do something you've time blocked, let's say it's 9AM and you're supposed to make some phone calls. But, at 9AM there's a knock on the door. What do you do? Before you do what you would normally do, write down where you feel the tightness/tension/whatever it is in your body that makes you want to do what you would normally do.

If I just lost you that's ok. This paragraph is for you... When you take habitual action on something, there is an intentional instruction or emotional driver given by the brain to the body's muscle to move. For example if I think of picking up a pen, instructions come from my brain to my fingers to pick up the pen. If I really want to pick up the pen, but I stop myself, I'll feel resistance. That resistance will show up, in this case, likely as tightness or tension in my arm or fingers. (I know, this is weirding you out. You've never thought about this before. That's ok. Neither has 80% or more of the population)((Yes, I guessed at that stat too.)

Ok, so let's go back to 9AM. You're at your desk about to make calls, when there's a knock on the door. What would you normally do? Yell, "Come in!", "Who's there?" or "Can I help you?" Whatever it is, before you do that, notice where the impulse to do that is in your body. It might be a furrow of the brow, or a tightening of the lips, or a knot in your stomach. Whatever it is, write it down first, and then do what you would normally do. Then, later in the day or whenever it's appropriate, go back

Business Ownership Mindset

to that feeling in your body and ask why you had to do what you normally do. The answer will come to you and from there you can figure out what you want to do with it.

It might be, because it might be important, or because it was weird because I work at home alone, or it might be something such as, "Because mom will get mad at me." If something totally left field shows up, that's ok. Follow the thought. You may find that Reason alone is enough to shut it down, or you might want to get into the emotion of it, or you might want to use repetition reminding yourself that the belief is old and doesn't work for you anymore. Regardless of what shows up, you now have more information and identify whether this belief is a successful belief for a business owner and you can change it!

Business Ownership Mindset

4. <u>**Now Go Do it.**</u>

So Sunday night you've set up a plan for the week and it's great. You get into the office Monday morning and something catastrophic happens and you're derailed first thing in the morning. Ask yourself, "Why would I let go of everything I've planned to take care of this? What is it that moves me to consider going off track?

> If the answer is something to the effect that, "This is my job, I'm paid to take care of this alligator." Great. Then dealing with the demands of the job is one thing, but the next question is, how do we make this alligator attack more predictable, or can we?

> If the answer is something to the effect that, "I really want this person to like me." Then you need to look at your need for approval.

> If the answer is something to the effect that, "This new item really is a higher priority and I need to readjust my schedule to account for it." Then readjust your calendar.

It really comes down to understanding your motivations, exploring your motivations and then weaving it back into how they play out in your day and how you would ideally want to run your day!

Now in order to ensure that you're not beating yourself up for not having stuck to a plan in the past, it's essential that you understand and take to heart that this whole exercise is a work in progress and to forgive yourself for not having stuck to the system in the past. Resenting the past or thinking that the past predicts the future is waste of your precious time and energy. It slows you down from moving forward. Just like a kid learning a new language, consider this practice and reassure yourself that you're getting better and better at this, even subtly, with every passing month.

And, by the way, I think forgiveness is a weird word, in that it's

Business Ownership Mindset

not like you did anything wrong, it's just a question of, is it time to let it go? And if the answer is yes, then you've forgiven yourself and you've let it go. We just don't have two words for that in English that I know of. If on the other hand you regret your actions and you're beating yourself up, then you do think you did something wrong, and it really is time to forgive yourself.

Now is the time to go and do it. Pull out your calendar. Pull out your list of big goals. And let's get these important time blocks into your calendar. If you have any questions about it please feel free to email me at info@AwarenessStrategies.com obligation free, or join us on social media and post your questions. I'm always looking to answer your questions and not just ramble. Please do help, to keep me giving you pertinent information to your business and send me your questions. Your questions are my red balloons. They make me happy and give me direction.

Business Ownership Mindset

Chapter 12
The Importance of Language and Your Self Talk

1. <u>You are your Head Cheerleader</u>

The enthusiasm, the passion and the joy that you find in your work HAS to come from you! It has to come from within you; internally. And your self-talk has to match that. Being able to zap the little negative thoughts that creep into your head is paramount. You have to be in control of that, because nobody else can be in control of that.

If you're looking externally for cheerleaders and you're driven by your external feedback, you're not going to be able to have the forward momentum that you need to make it through the tough times. You can't be wasting your time diverting other people's judgement but more importantly you need to realize that the internal drive won't be there until you make sure it's there.

Let me give you a left field example and maybe it'll make more sense. Have you ever met someone, (yes it's usually girls who do this, but not always), who is really good looking but they think they're ugly. And as often as you can you keep trying to assure them of how good looking they are, but they don't believe it. Sadly, there is nothing you can say that will sway them, (although repetition is a great teacher) they need to question why they are so emotionally attached to the idea that they're ugly before any of those heart felt pleas will land, allowing them to believe that you think they're good looking.

The same thing happens in business. You have to believe that you are competent and capable in business before anything anyone says is going to be able to land and allow you to believe that your clients and others think that you're good in business. You have to take a solid look at

Business Ownership Mindset

your beliefs and ensure that you at least have 51% of your beliefs in favour of you succeeding. Of course I'd recommend this was WAY higher than that, but you at least want to make sure that you can tip the scale in your favour when you need it. After all, isn't that the whole purpose of cheerleaders? To rile up the crowd when the team needs the push the most?

Not only do you need to know that you have just a little more energy left, and a little more enthusiasm left, and a little more passion left when you think you've run out, but you'll need to know that you have a jet pack in your back pocket that you can use when you need it most, to get through times when you think you're out of energy. Business has a way of breaking you down to force you to build yourself up so that you can see what you're really made of. And if you don't insist on hiring your own team of mental cheerleaders before you need them, then you best be prepared to pay a steeper salary when you need them. ;)

It's WAY easier to get them in place ahead of time than it is to wait until you need encouragement to start mustering it up then. So, do it now. It's as good a time as any.

Business Ownership Mindset

2. <u>The Path of Least Resistance</u>

It's always easier to take the path of least resistance, but if it's so much fun building and growing your dreams, why do old patterns return to take over, AGAIN?

It kind of comes back to the notion that I referred to in the past sections, when we look at doing something that moves us forward, but it's out of our comfort zone. It's usually out of our comfort zone because it's a new skill and we're not as good at is as we are at other skills that we've mastered. We know from experience that when we do things we've mastered that we get a certain kind of feedback and if that feedback makes us feel good, such as having people like us, then of course it's going to be easier to fall back on the old habit.

Whether it's around business, golf or otherwise, it's very tempting to take the path of least resistance. It just feels better than the uncomfortable path of growth.

I think it's important to note that people have tendencies, when it comes to learning, that are deeply engrained. We learn from a young age how to respond to the learning curve. If we got rewarded for doing things well rather than learning new things, then we learn that it's better to know than it is to learn. If we were encouraged when we 'failed' then we learned that it's better to learn than to know. All of this is going to come into play in our adult life. It's unavoidable; it's now a belief we've engrained and a skill we've learned well. The good news is we can always change our learned behaviours, if we choose to.

Business Ownership Mindset

3. Now Go Do it.

Changing your self-talk can be daunting and it can be easy. It usually depends on the time of day as to which one you find yourself in. However, the more you understand the importance of inner confidence (not arrogance) and solution oriented attitudes, the easier it will be to maintain control of your inner game.

If you find yourself constantly taking a step backward in your business, ask yourself, what are the underlying commonalities and how can you shift that?

Ask yourself, are you just going after a feeling of success or are you going after a feeling of being authentic and true to your aspirations?

Finding and dissecting repeating patterns can be an extremely useful way to uncover hidden sabotage and letting it go. Knowing where you want to go and continually taking steps to move you forward in the planning AND implementation of the plan is extremely useful way to keep yourself on track and identifying self-sabotage.

Chapter 13
Creating a Philosophy that works for you

1. **<u>Social Acceptance (Political Correctness and why it'll be the death of you)</u>**

You cannot worry about what other people think about you. Well, you can, but it's not only a waste of energy, its soul sucking. You have to know that there is going to be a judgement on you, there has to be, that's how human's function to survive. They are always judging their surroundings. You have to understand that they judge based on their past experience and their past has nothing to do with your present. They've created their judgement somewhere else. It was with them long before you came along and it'll be with them long after you're gone.

Now you may think that Political Correctness is being sensitive to the group consciousness and how they respond and how they feel whereas sacred cows might be a better way of looking at this, and sacred cows is the idea that 'what people say' is important but they don't why. So are we challenging PC or Sacred Cows? And my answer is yes. Partially because I think PC is becoming a sacred cow. We're justifying people's sensitivity as MY issue that I have to walk gingerly around but we never question why YOU think it's a sensitive issue?

This isn't really about challenging people and the way THEY are, so much as it is about understanding why YOU do what YOU do and not taking people's unquestioned sensitivity personally.

Another word for all of this might be Social Norms. We create social norms and then we need to break them.

Business Ownership Mindset

The example I use in class is this. Say, Mary, was a prospect of yours and you had a meeting with her and the day you had a meeting with her, you announced yourself at the office, her assistant brought you in through the maze of cubicles and pointed at her door and said, "Go ahead and walk right in, she's expecting you." So you walk over to the door, open it and announce yourself, at which point Mary jumps out of her chair, screams and yells, "Get out!!"

Now, if this happened to you, what would your first reaction be? How would you feel? What would you do? I'm sure we can only guess at this, because this exact thing hasn't happened, but at the same time, we kind of know because similar enough things have happened to us.

So you think what you think, you feel what you feel and you react the way you react. Question for you; is the way you react because of Mary? Or is it because of other incidents in the past that you've remembered and you're partially judging this situation on?

And secondly, what if Mary reacted the way she did because two years previously she got mugged in a back alley, by surprise, by someone wearing a black turtle neck just like the one you were wearing the day you walked in her office? Did her reaction have anything to do with you personally? No, of course not. And is there any way you could have possibly known that when you decided to wear that shirt on that day? Of course not! But if you allow yourself to feel rejected by her reaction you're not just letting Mary run your business, you're letting some thug in some back alley run your business! And your life for that matter.

Obviously, from an outsiders perspective, you didn't mean to hurt Mary nor did she mean to hurt you, but if you allow other people's judgement to affect you then you're going to walk away hurt and likely never give Mary the opportunity to do business with you again.

I want you to understand that everything you do has about as much relevance in anyone else's life as that black turtle neck. What you

Business Ownership Mindset

say, what you do, how you act all has the exact same amount of relevance as that black turtle neck. None of it originated with you and you can't control them.

Some people will say, "Well, OBVIOUSLY, it didn't have anything to do with me, I didn't even say anything."

Ok let's suppose you said something, such as "Hi, Are you Mary? I was told just to walk right in."

What if that caused Mary to freak out because in her mind, you shouldn't just barge into someone's office. Then you think about it and come to the conclusion that she's right and from then on in you refuse to walk into a door until someone on the other side gives you permission to walk through the door way. It all sounds gentle enough, but if that did happen, you just allowed someone's past to dictate your future without you even knowing why!

This happens all day every day to some people. They walk on egg shells trying not to upset anyone around them and all they end up doing is making themselves a walking wreckage.

To make an even stronger example although it's probably the more subtle examples that take people's confidence away, let's say I wanted to wear skirt suits to the office. I may get a barrage of feedback saying that it's inappropriate for a woman to wear a skirt in the boardroom because it's flaunting her sexuality. Personally I call bullshit, completely. I believe that a person has to be authentic to themselves and be able to express themselves in harmony with the way they think. I'm not saying showing up in the boardroom in lingerie is the way to go, but I am saying that the individual needs to decide what is truly in their repertoire of being honest and in integrity is essential.

Some will argue that you can't distract people in the boardroom. I laugh because most people in the boardroom are looking for anything to distract them because most meetings aren't held with focus and attention

Business Ownership Mindset

in mind. If they were, more would get done. If the meetings are intriguing enough to keep your mind entertained then one; that really has nothing to do with the way people dress and two;

Maybe I can look at this and ask myself, how do I become more intellectually intriguing and how do I become more able to lock into your intelligence to accomplish the purpose of the meeting, but I can only take on my part of it, not your part of it.

There are perceptions that people have as to the way that people around them "should" behave and I'm saying that most of them are crap, but more importantly there is NOTHING you can do about someone else's preconceived notions of what is appropriate or inappropriate, what is right and what is wrong, what is socially acceptable and what isn't what is the way they think you should behave and what isn't.

Obviously, if there's a dress code in the office and you've agreed to adhere to it then adhere to it. But, I'm not talking about dress codes, rules of etiquette or abuse. I'm talking about taking people's previously established bias or judgement and the importance of letting it fall off of you like water on a ducks back.

You must learn to not take people's judgement personally, because it's not yours to take.

And for the record, I get it; there are social norms in business settings. Once upon a time everyone wore three piece suits, then two piece suits, then it was ok to wear short sleeve shirts and khakis and they became the norm. And really it doesn't matter what the dress code is men just aren't as sexy as women are. Women are way more fun to look at. I get that. ☺

Seriously though, there are going to be things that you don't say or do because of the consequences of those behaviours and yes you want to weigh those out, but what would be most beneficial is to look internally and let go of the negative attachment that you may have to someone

Business Ownership Mindset

else's reaction. As long as there is a negative attachment for you that is attached to their reaction to your behaviour the original source of your emotional reaction is going to rule your behaviour instead of you, and that's not good.

And, vice versa! Regardless of how somebody else behaves, it's my perception of how I think they should behave that needs to be kyboshed. And, yes I'll have boundaries, but those boundaries dictate how I behave not how I expect someone else to behave. And again I'm not talking about illegal behaviour, just day to day normal interactions. If I am offended by what other people say, I'm going to spend my entire day being offended. It's too easy to live that way. It sucks, but it's easy. I can always find someone who will say something offensive! But, if I get rid of that judgement in myself, then and only can can I chose to find a way to take everything someone says as a compliment or at least as a neutral comment and that is much more challenging, but it's also a WAY more fun way to live. Some people may say that's a delusional way of living but I believe it's delusional to think that people thought about you before they said what they said. They're just going on routine, so why not think of it as them trying to keep you safe, or them trying to compliment you or them giving you attention, because really under it all that is what they're doing.

Let me put this another way: Two people reading this chapter are going to take it two completely different ways. What I say has absolutely no effect on how you hear me. And likewise what you say has no effect on how I hear it. How I've been raised and how I've been taught, and what I've learned along the way creates my perception. And that perception is going to bias everything I ever see, hear, taste, touch and smell. Hence, if I learned that when someone walks into the room and they say hi that it's a sign of familiarity and if they say hello it's a sign of formality and you as a stranger walk in and say hi, and I think, "Well, that was kind of rude." That has nothing to do with you. Nothing! Zero, nadda, zip!

Business Ownership Mindset

At this point you may be thinking that there are multiple levels to this and different levels of severity, but I believe it applies to all levels. There's consequential and inconsequential, there's corporate and there's running your own business, there's building your own business up and not getting sued. I agree and this chapter alone could be a book unto itself. So start where you see that it makes sense. Find the lowest level that you see your perception of other people's reactions slowing you down from building on your goals and dreams and work on diffusing your reactions.

Think of yourself at the cockpit of a 747 with buttons all over the place, and if people are pushing your buttons I'd like you to recognize that they are your button. If you like it, great! Keep it! Maybe even reinforce it! Take some more wire and make sure that button is easily set off! But if you don't like it, diffuse it. It's your button. And at the same time recognize that other people have their buttons. And just because you pushed one, it doesn't mean that it's your fault. It's their button and you have to accept that they are going to have buttons and as they connect with you for whatever reason, some of those buttons are going to get pushed and you cannot control whether they like having that button pushed, they hate it, or that theirs is wired differently than yours. All you can do is open up communication and attempt to figure it out, if you so choose. But know that you're not obligated to.

Another way of looking at this is to ask why are we afraid?

Why are we afraid of moving forward?

There's a philosophy in our society that says, "If I just live the Victorian lifestyle, I'll be happy." And that's not true. In fact nothing could be further than the truth.

It says, "If I just don't step on anybody else's toes, I'll be happy."

"If I just don't offend anybody, I'll be happy."

"If I just don't step out of line, everybody will be happy."

Business Ownership Mindset

"If you just do what I ask you to do, we'll both be happy."

That's a complete CROCK! It doesn't work AT ALL!

At the same time, I can't be offended every time I offend somebody else or I'm going to be walking on egg shells all day. I'm going to be terrified of my own shadow.

I have to be able to accept the idea that they created that resistance in themselves long before I came along and they're going to have it long after I leave. I cannot be responsible for them freaking out just because I'm 'wearing a black turtleneck'. I can't be responsible for their reaction just because I look a certain way, or I do a certain thing or I say a certain thing. I mean really look at me. I can't be responsible for people freaking out because of the length of my hair, the length of my nails and the height of my shoes. People's reactions are their reactions, and their reason for their reactions is their issue.

I have to be able to let go of their resistance. I have to be able to let go of my own resistance and I have to consciously know, why I'm doing what I'm doing and not just use the excuse of "it's the right way to do it."

I'm not doing it because I'm looking for love in all the wrong places, I'm doing it because I want shock value, I want attention and I want it now. I'm doing it to an extreme to give people permission to do it at all! Whatever it is that's going on for someone who is afraid, we can let go of it and we can laugh and say it's ok. You know you can do it with me because I've done it first. I consciously see why I do what I do, and I know what it is, so when people react they don't hit a negative button in me. They can react and we can laugh about it because I'm not getting defensive or reactionary, I'm observing them and I'm giving them permission to react in whatever way they do. And what that allows me to do is to, in this example, then build a brand around myself, I can build my marketing around it, I can build a company around it that says, "It's ok to be who you are, in fact come follow us and we'll show you how to do it."

Business Ownership Mindset

I give people permission to do it, because I've done it myself. And, I've done it such a loud way that you can't help but notice that I've done it.

But, I never would have been able to do that if I were constantly afraid of what other people thought, or say or do when they're around me. Some love it, some like it, some couldn't care less, some are offended and some hate it. And that's ok. I welcome all of those reactions.

My favourite reaction was my mother's reaction to seeing my nails one day. My dad asked to see my nails so I showed him and my mother, who was standing beside him, couldn't help herself but blurted out, "They're hideous!"

I laughed so hard, I couldn't stop myself. Yes, there was an element of sincerity, but there was also an element of self-preservation and it all hit me as hilarious. I finally said, "That was a great reaction! Thank you!"

She had no idea why someone would want that kind of reaction, but when we talked through it she realized that it's my job to get people to question their reactions. It's my job to snap people out of their generational habits. Now, I understand that your job with your company might not be to snap people awake, but I also understand that without standing up and giving yourself the power to be you, you aren't going to be able to attract the right kind of clients to your company in order to make the vast amount of money that you deserve to make. When you're being authentic in yourself, meaning that you know why you do what you do and you want to do it, you'll know how to deal with people when they do their thing. You'll know that it's got nothing to do with you . Then, if someone gets offended, you can simply say, "That seemed like it offended you."

And you can have a real conversation after that. You might say, "I can appreciate that it seemed offensive, but I didn't mean to offend you.

Business Ownership Mindset

It doesn't get into an "Elevator Argument" as I like to call them. And when you're grounded and you can push people's buttons for the right reasons, you'll attract to you a solid following of super loyal clients. And you cannot do that by gingerly trying to avoid walking on proverbial egg shells. It doesn't work.

Business Ownership Mindset

2. **Multiple ways to think successfully.**

Know first off that your results are your results. They're not someone else's. They are yours.

She didn't walk into anyone else's boardroom, she walked into mine. So in that moment, knowing what's going on for me is all that really matters.

In order to "think successfully" the most powerful way to do that is through introspection and to let go of the resistance toward the negativity. I know that may seem soft, but it's actually the opposite. Anger, bitter and vengeance may sound powerful but they only lead to short term solutions. Don't get me wrong, I'm an advocate for anger. It's a great emotion for short powerful bursts of energy. It can be great for getting the house clean or running a sprint. Long term, however, it's not sustainable without injury. It's an emotion to express not a lifestyle strategy.

By letting go of negativity you start to see things from a place of "it just is". It's a very neutral place. From this space it makes it much easier to make decisions pragmatically or simply functionally. One of the reasons that this is more powerful is that you now have the choice to construct or deconstruct the situation in front of you. With a negative hold, you really only have one option. With a neutral positioning you now have essentially infinite possibilities of how you want to respond from here. From here there are good choice, great choices, risky choices and baffling choices. No one choice is the right choice, however, at least you get to decide.

It may seem odd that there isn't one single way to think in order to become successful, but if you look at a spectrum of people you perceive as successful, you'll notice that they don't all act or think the same way. And, the important thing for you isn't that you need to think

Business Ownership Mindset

the way someone else does or that the way you are now is somehow wrong. Think of it like flowers. Maybe right now your mindset is still in the budding stages and you're looking around at all of these other flowers that have blossomed. They're all different and you're going to be different from them, but you will eventually blossom. Whether you're following a mentor, reading the classics, or even while you're reading this book, you're going to find ideas that move you. Simply pick the one that moves you most and run with that idea until it becomes a habit. Then pick the next milestone or attitude that you want to aim for and practice it until it becomes a habit. That way you're constantly letting go of beliefs that no longer serve you and adapting to those that you want to grow into. By doing that, the path you take is unique to you, but at the same time easier than bushwhacking your way to success. The way you know that a philosophy is right for you, is by asking yourself, "Does this idea serve and support me? Is it important for me right now?"

Business Ownership Mindset

3. <u>Figuring out what's important for you.</u>

I know a lot of people have very solid definitions of what's important to them and that's great! If you're one of those people, run with it! You're off to the races! However, if you're not one of those people or you're starting to notice that what you thought was important to you seems to be hindering more than it's helping you may want to ponder this idea for a while. Ask yourself, "Does this serve and support me?"

Just because a concept is easy to work with or it feels good doing it, doesn't mean that it supports you. Just because an idea is socially acceptable or because your parents taught you to think that way, doesn't mean that it supports you. Really, the way you know if something serves and supports you is by looking at your goals, asking where you want to go and what you want to achieve, and does it fit within your values.

Now the confusion begins. How can something be important to me and not fit into my values? How do I know what do if I set a goal, but achieving it is going to contradict my values? And, no these contradictions don't have to be monumental; they can be small and insidious, or small and insignificant. How do you tell? Introspection. A lot of introspection. The only person who has the answer to these questions is you. And the only way you know you're on track is by continually having conversations with yourself to find the answers. You know, most people are better acquainted with their enemies than they are with themselves. Most people just don't get to know themselves, so even by doing that you're ahead in the game.

To give you an example of this I've had many clients whose biggest challenge was balancing kids and careers. And, I most certainly get it. There's only 24 hours in a day, most things happen in 8 of them and without money the kids don't function and without kids the money

Business Ownership Mindset

doesn't function. First you want to look at your long term goals, in this case in the area of money and kids. What do you want to accomplish? And it may be that the two are seemingly completely contradictory, such as I want to work 40 hours a week in the office and I want to home school my kids. That is not my goal, just an example. ☺ If that were the case, obviously you can't be in two places at once, but what you might be able to do is have someone else home school the kids. Or homeschool them after work. Start brainstorming all the possible ways to make it happen without judging or shutting down the ideas. Remember, they're only ideas at this point. No one is acting on any of them yet. Once you've brainstormed you may find that brilliant balance that you were looking for.

In the end, you may have to move a very important meeting with the president of Coke Cola because your twelve year old will never be in the twelve year old's finals again and it can't be moved. Yes, the meeting with Coke Cola can be moved, when it's important enough.

The successful philosophy that you bring to your life isn't necessarily in what you decide on; it's in the open-mindedness with which you decide.

Business Ownership Mindset

4. **Tools and Tricks**

First when making a decision, whether it's about creating your philosophy, or figuring out what projects to take on, I cannot emphasize how important it is to get rid of your resistance or negative feelings first. If you don't get rid of the negativity you run into "ground hog day" syndrome; same issues, different day.

Get rid of the negativity so you can make decisions from a place of neutrality. More on this in the next section.

Second allow yourself to brainstorm without censorship. Write out all of the possibilities no matter how silly they are. In fact I'll often start a brainstorming session with something like 'train circus squirrels to do it', just so that I have the silliest one on the page and everything seems valid after that.

Once you've brainstormed, if you haven't come up with the brilliant idea yet, take the idea that obviously won't work and turn it on its head so that it's even more ridiculous. Ridiculous ideas have a way of spawning creativity.

Once you have some ideas that might work. Decide on your plan and run with it. This is the part where you practice being decisive. Not because you know it's the right choice, but because it's the best choice you can make right now with the information that you have. And that, is as good as it gets some days.

Just because something happens along the way that says a different way would have been better, doesn't mean that you derail and jump tracks. Stick to your plan and run it to fruition. You'll be amazing with the results that tenacity can create.

Business Ownership Mindset

5. Now Go Do it.

First things first; get rid of the resistance. Going back to our example in PC will be the death of you: To get rid of the resistance that we feel when we push someone else's buttons, we can start to ask ourselves, why do I feel that way? Is it because they remind me of someone else? Is it because of something happening somewhere else in my life? We can do a lot of introspection on the cause of the feeling and simply by understanding the origin of these issues we can often let go of them. I believe that Success Therapy is the way to go, or you may even have another method that you like to use. Either way, I recommend that you work on whatever might be going on for you that's impeding your success.

Another exercise you'll want to do is to write down;

"I'll be happy when person X does this…",

"I'll be happy when person Y does that…", and

"I'll be happy when person Z does the other thing…."

Now notice where in those items are you doing something?

What is it that you can do to be happy?

When you have it so that your list is 80% of you doing things to make you happy and less than 20% of your external environment to make you happy, to me that is when you're moving in the right direction. You want to move to '100% of everything that I do makes me happy and my external environment is irrelevant.'

Understanding how I control my reaction to what 'she's wearing' or my reaction to 'the way he's driving' allows me to have 100% awareness of what my reactions are to my external environment.

If I'm happy with my reaction, I'll keep doing it. If I'm not happy

Business Ownership Mindset

with it, knowing that I have control over my reaction, I can change it.

It's not, "If you didn't wear that outfit, I'd be more comfortable."

Once you've figured out your reaction to your external circumstances, or even while you're figuring it out, figure out what's important for you. Knowing what is important for you, you can even further narrow in your attention and you become even more powerful with your actions!

Getting rid of resistance you have toward doing certain actions, like accounting or prospecting, filing or figuring out software, can be done in a very similar way. I chose those four examples because it usually takes four very different personality types to do those four jobs, so odds are you'll like one or two of them and you'll dislike one or two of them. In other words, no one likes doing everything. Breathe. You're human. And, when you find yourself facing a daunting task that makes you question your competence or your intelligence, breathe. It's only because somewhere in the past you took on this task before and something went awry. Let it go (through reason, meditation, Success Therapy, or your choice of modality) and know that curiosity will get you through this. As questions like what if it was fun? What if it was easy for me? How can I make this fun and easy for me? Remember, your brain is a problem solving machine. Give it great questions and it'll give you great answers. We're in the section of creating a successful philosophy, so go write down some points that you've found useful and pick the one concept that you want to embody and put into action a plan for thinking, feeling, believing, or acting that way.

Business Ownership Mindset

Chapter 14
Strategy vs Tactics

1. Big Picture, little picture, what begins with a picture?

In business a lot of entrepreneurs think very tactically. They're busy most of the time thinking, "I need to do this", or "I need to do that."

Let's start with; "What is a goal?" and "What is an objective?" This may seem like semantics and it somewhat is, but the importance of semantics is being able to be as clear about the message as possible to attempt to limit the gap between what I say and what you hear.

It's like having a mission statement for your company, knowing what your mission statement is and having everyone at every educational level within your company knowing what the mission statement is and how it affects them and their jobs. It can't be using precocious words and involve ambiguity. (Like that sentence did.)

It has to make sense to everyone at every level to have one cohesive mission. Likewise when it comes to goals, objectives, strategies and tactics you want to know what you're dealing with and eliminate the ambiguity. When it comes to communicating your strategies it has to be at a level that everyone understands or it can quickly become undermined.

So there are a few pictures that you'll want to have in place for your company so that everyone, especially you, can see where your company is going. In my humble opinion, you'll want to start with the big picture. However if you've already started with the small picture, that's ok too! At least you got started!! From here, let's get a big picture established.

Business Ownership Mindset

>You're biggest picture is going to be your **mission statement**. It will be the most generalized statement for your company. It will in simple terms define the culture of your company and the impact you want it to have in the world.

>You're next biggest picture will be your **vision statement**. This will articulate what you want the company to look like at its greatest; whether that's the furthest out that you can see, or the most functional that you can see it.

The above are simply statements, usually one or two lines that are intended to move people to act in a cohesive manner towards those outcomes in all of their daily tasks.

>**Goals** on the other hand are much more specific. You might have one year goals, five year goals and even 20 year goals; all of which you should have. These will be milestones or achievements that for the most part you don't have a clue how to accomplish them. If you know how to accomplish them, I would define that as a task.

>There can be big **tasks**, even huge tasks, but if you know how to do them then they are tasks not goals. The purpose of a goal is not only to grow your company but to grow you as an individual. It's meant to test you, tender you and build you into something that at this point you can only aspire to be. As I'm sure you know, goals are specific measurements that you plan on achieving by a certain time.

>**Affirmations and declarations**, just as a point of interest here, are supportive statements used to help you achieve a goal. They're usually very generalized and are very useful statements, but they are not goals. "We treat every client with respect" is an affirmation or a declaration, or maybe even a tag line, but it's not a goal.

>**Objectives**, to me, are not interchangeable with goals. An objective is more the underlying reason for the goal. For example the goal might be to have international offices within five years. The

Business Ownership Mindset

objective is to have international offices with five years so that we can help people in multiple languages and offer resources to even more people. In this example, the goal is international offices; the objective is to serve in multiple languages with a greater client base.

> **Strategy** is looking at the goal and considering the ways in which we might be able to accomplish the goal and not from a "doing" position, but from a "why" position. Asking questions such as "Why do we want to go international?", "Why would we want different languages?", "Why do we want Spanish?" and of course, a whole string of others.

>**Tactics** is looking at the strategy and then asking, "How are we going to do that?" Now, you get to dig into what needs to happen and when. Now, it makes sense! Now, you have all your energy going into a very specific direction for a very specific reason. Through this complete succession of thought, you'll find that your actions are much more successful and fruitful.

Once your goals are in place, I want you to be able to transition from a tactical way of thinking into a strategic way of thinking quickly and habitually. But it, like any other skill, is quickly turned by the wayside if you don't know what the benefit of it is and why you'd go through the awkward learning curve to pursue this thing called strategy.

The good news is that you may agree that it's important and you set aside time every month for it, but then the question comes, what are you really doing in that time to be effectively working on strategy.

The bad news is that you may think you're too small of a company to think strategically. But, you're not. Even if the only people in that meeting are you, yourself and you; strategy meetings are essential to your growth. And, when you do set up those meetings, you want to know what it is that you're going to be working on in that meeting in order to really strategize for your company. Even though you may sell widgets and you feel you'll always be selling widgets, there has to be a strategy for

Business Ownership Mindset

getting your widgets out to market. You want to be asking yourself, "How am I going to grow the company?", "Do I want to get into different markets?" and, "How am I going to go into different markets?"

I guess before we go there we need to ask, "What is a Strategic Thinking question?" and, "What is a tactical thinking question?"

Business Ownership Mindset

2. **Strategical Thinking and Tactical Thinking**

Tactical Thinking is all about what you're actually going to do; it's about specific actions and detailed information on how to do something.

Strategic Thinking is all about why you're looking at doing the thing before you even concern yourself with what the thing is.

Just to keep this simple; Tactical Thinking is about picking up a bike and learning to ride it. Strategic Thinking is about asking why you want to learn to ride a bike, deciding based on your environment and height what kind of bike would be the easiest to learn on and looking into who the best teacher would be to teach you how to learn how to ride a bike.

Most of us just grabbed our WAY over sized hand-me-down bike, blindly agreed to get support from our sadistic siblings and held on tight as they pushed us down the hill.

That wasn't most of us? That was just me? Oh, well then I guess you can see why a little strategic thinking might have given me a better foundation for my formative bicycling years.

And, Yes! It's much easier to see the folly in other people's way of thinking.

And, Yes! You can only strategize for so long and eventually you have to get on the bike and push the pedals. In fact, you'll spend A LOT more time pushing the pedals than strategizing.

Business Ownership Mindset

3. **Why you need to be thinking Strategically**

a. You can't grow the company without it, and

b. If the market changes whether temporarily or permanently you're going to have to figure out how to deal with that change, and in order for that conversation to be effective it has to be strategically based.

Change is inevitable, but when you don't see it coming, you're lost. As humans we have a tendency to think that 'this' is the way that it's always going to be. We don't even consider that people everywhere are planning on how to make the most stable fundamentals in our lives change and that one day, it will all change! It's kind of like how in my 20's I couldn't care less about politics because I didn't think that anything they did affected me. And now I laugh and I laugh hard because I realize that everything they do affects me.

Business Ownership Mindset

4. Pay Grade appropriate Strategizing

Once you start thinking strategically you'll start noticing that there's a strategy to everything, but that doesn't mean you have to be a part of that. Strategizing for what markets you want to go into and how you're going to do it is your job. Strategizing for what kind of cards you're going to send out for your clients' birthdays is probably not your job. Even if you're a solopreneur, that decision could be made by a virtual assistant and should be. For every 15 minutes you spend making a 15$/hour decision, you're losing out on making 100$ or maybe even 5000$ depending on your pay grade. 15 minutes may not seem like much to you, until you pass it by and you can't get it back again. If the decisions being made aren't directly effecting the goals of the company, delegate those decisions. Spend your time on Revenue Generating Activity and leave the rest for someone else. Especially if you have a team of people!

Chapter 15
How to Strategize

1. **Setting up time to do it; NGDI**

Within your company, if you haven't read it already, you will want to set up a strategy meeting for yourself at least once a month. I know some people think it's ridiculous to set it up that frequently, but some people think it's ridiculous to set them up that infrequently. If you're not in the habit of meeting monthly for a strategy meeting, set them up. Start with an hour even if it's only, you and yourself that are showing up for it.

Ideally I would book this for a whole day and ideally out of the office. Being able to get into a strategic, long term mindset isn't the easiest thing for a lot of people to do, and it is quite different that day to day tactical thinking. Being able to get out of your normal work space can help to focus you, but don't use it as a distraction or an opportunity to avoid.

Business Ownership Mindset

2. What to do in that time; NGDI

I have a lot of people tell me that they booked their strategy meeting, the time came and they stared at the time block in their calendar having no idea what to do in this time. I can appreciate that. So, let's look at what you have. You have your 20, 10, 5 and 1 year goals. You have your legacy, mission and vision statements and values. You have your culture, your work environment, and your systems. You have your ideal client, your brand and a list of projects. Now is the time that we're going to figure out what you're going to do, by figuring out how all of these pieces fit together. During your strategy meeting you're going to be thinking about and reviewing, which markets you're going into, how you're going to get to market, and what you do when you get there. I know that may sound overly simplified and each one of those questions is covered in a library of books unto themselves, but you need to start somewhere. Writing those questions in the details of your meeting is a good place to start.

If you already do strategy meetings and you already have a team of people that you work with then you'll want to make sure that those meetings are as useful as possible and that every time you have them that they end with actionable item lists for the people involved that they know what they're doing, why they're doing it and that it works in conjunction with the work they already have on the go, and if not why not, and what takes precedence.

It may sound nonsensical to say that or that a strategy meeting should be a strategy meeting and not a planning meeting, but I can't tell you how many meetings I've sat in on that were totally useless let alone how many more I've heard about. In your Strategy Meeting you want to be asking yourself the big overshadowing questions. Some of those questions might be; Where does my ideal client spend their time, what's the easiest way to get a hold of them. Do I want them to take action when

Business Ownership Mindset

I get a hold of them? Do I want to stick in their mind and take action later? Is there a way to double dip on their attention or can I get their attention twice in a short period of time?

Of course these answers will vary vastly depending on the size of your corporation, whether you sell services or products, whether their high end, specific market or mass market. But regardless of which market you're going into there's always a big picture game and a detailed game being played out. The more clearly you can see that big picture and share that vision with your team, the easier it will be for them to make tactical choices. You'll be narrowing down their scope for them and their parameters will be easier to see.

Business Ownership Mindset

3. Allocating Tasks; NGDI

Let's talk about articulating your strategy to your team. If it's you, yourself and you, the task allocation is pretty easy. You're just going to have to figure out when you're going to do it! We'll talk about making sure it actually gets done in the next section.

If you have a team then deciding who's going to do what is your next challenge.

I'd like to say, "Obviously, if you have your teams in place like your COO, CMO and CIO in place that you can simply delegate to them." I'd like to say that, but I have yet to see a company where it happens that smoothly. Sometimes delegation is a beautiful thing, but there are always going to be times when those lines get blurred. And, if you don't have those people in place then it can be even more cumbersome. For the most part certain jobs are obviously IT and some are obviously marketing but for those times when the lines do get blurred it's going to require some conversation with personality and skill set assessment. Sometimes it would just be easier to give the job to one person, but it makes more sense to have the right department learn how to do it.

Once you have an overarching strategy, articulating that strategy to your team clearly and more importantly getting their buy in will be paramount. Please don't tell me you just heard, "I'm the boss they'll do what I tell them to do", in your head. Even if you are that kind of boss, if your team doesn't get what you're trying to accomplish, they can't implement it. And until they get it, they can't buy into it. It's not their job to get it. It's your job to ensure they got it.

Some people really like detailed plans so that they know exactly what you mean. Other people can't stand detailed plans and they won't do it to the detail that you've defined. Yes, you guessed it, it's up to you to figure out how they like being communicated to and communicating to

Business Ownership Mindset

them in that way. Yes, I get that you may think you should just fire anyone who doesn't listen to you the way you speak, and you're more than welcome to do that. Before you do, you might want to know that kind of thinking will be extremely costly. It'll cost you in hiring, training, and creative growth. There's a less expensive more beneficial way that yes, will require you to change, but really isn't that what we've been talking about this entire time? You can make the investment in you and it'll pay off dividends forever, or you can spend your time, money and resources on hiring, training and firing people. The choice is yours.

I'm going to assume you're on board, or at least willing to find out how to be on board, which for this exercise is good enough. You see, throughout this entire book, I've been giving you the pros and the cons for each argument and an example of how it could work. Sometimes I give you examples of why other ways don't work. By doing so you get to engage your linear or logical mind and your metaphorical mind, which by the way is just as logical, however it demonstrates itself in a different way. One side likes pros and cons the other side likes stories. Giving you both in a book, allows you to find the information you need to make a choice. If I were to work with you I'd have a better idea of what that ratio is for you. It might be 50/50 or it might be 100/0 or 0/100. My job isn't to get you information and be done with it. My job is to say it as many different ways as I need to in order for you to have an epiphany and see things in a way that you never saw it before. My job is essentially that of the CEO to management and getting you to buy into an idea so that you then take action on it, because when you do that, my vision comes to life through you. If we were working together right now, I'd ask you if it makes sense to you and ask you what you're going to implement, what you're going to quit doing that you've been doing and what you need more clarity on. But at this point, I'm going to let you take care of that on your own.

Business Ownership Mindset

4. **Accountability; NGDI**

In strategizing and tactics you came up with a plan and how you're going to do it. Now the question is how do you stay accountable and actually do it, so you're not just jumping from one idea to the next saying, "Oh we'll do this! And we'll do this! AND, now we'll do this!" And none of it ever gets done. To be able to put in place markers and deadlines saying, "This will be done by this date and if I don't have it done by then what are the consequences?" Also just as importantly, knowing what the benefits to getting it done and at that time are.

If you have a team of people you want to be able to tell your executives not only to go do "this, that and the other thing" but you also want to ensure that you have buy in. They need to know about it, buy into it and agree to their own timelines, benefits and consequences otherwise you're coming back to them asking why they didn't get it done and they're going, "Get what done?"

Knowing how you measure your progress is very important. For example a friend of mine, Shamir, was very good at this. He put aside a list of tasks telling his maintenance team, "This is the list of things we need to do. Know that when you maintain the equipment, things last longer and we'll spend less money on equipment long term, obviously. But, there's also the safety component. If you don't maintain the equipment and it goes faulty someone could get hurt. " So, management was saying, this is the work that needs to get done and then they put it out to the field. The field guys are getting capital work telling them that their work needs to get done. New builds were telling them that they needed work done. And then, there was other operational stuff that needed to get done. They were being bombarded from three different directions. They ended up just prioritizing what they felt was a priority in a given day. Shamir felt their pain and he got the three groups together. Don't kid yourself, they went in kicking and screaming. Their managers

Business Ownership Mindset

went in kicking and screaming, but he got them into a room together and said, "I'm going to echo your concerns. Here's what I hear. You aren't getting your work done and here is the other department's concerns and here are my concerns. Now let's put them all together and coordinate this work. In the end he drove them together to come up with a plan that worked. They would then meet together on a monthly basis. Then he said, "Here's what we're going to do. We're going to have this dashboard that's going to show the progress of your commitment that you settled on. You met together and you all agreed, it wasn't my plan, I wasn't even in that meeting." In fact no managers were in that meeting only the supervisors and the crew leaders got together and they decided on what they were going to do. He simply told them, "Listen generously and to balance your needs with everyone else's needs. Because I don't want to hear from there, that if an escalation comes to me, and I see that you've been uncivil in that meeting, it's going to reflect on your performance. You come back and say to me, these are the risks and these are the benefits and I'll say no problem. I accept those risks." They all agreed to do it, then we needed to find a way to track it. The field guys were going to track how well they did. Just by keeping a dashboard, they were driven by the priorities that they themselves owned up to. If it ever went sideways, he would hear from his guys because they were meeting every month and they would say to the field guys, "We agreed that this is the way you wanted to do it, why didn't you do it?" And if something out of the ordinary happened he would hear about it and he would go and talk to whoever took them away from their plan. Because they agreed to it, they stuck to their plans. The only time it didn't work is when someone from another division took them off plan.

Then Shamir could go and ask why they were taken off course and they could figure out a way to bring them all together again and say, "Let's fix this."

He held his counter management accountable and that dashboard

Business Ownership Mindset

became the most valuable asset and in fact it became the crowning glory of that department and they would wave a flag to the successes it brought to the company. In the end they forgot who started the idea but that's ok, because it became their idea. They owned it as their own and that's why it worked so well. They bought into it 100%.

The real question here is how does this apply to you and what can you measure?

Business Ownership Mindset

Chapter 16
Support

1. **Setting up a team**

At last the evolution of the vision, involving other people. At some point we want to move from creating a vision in isolation to involving other people. For some it might mean creating a vision that is community centred and I believe that if your vision is big enough it will always be community centred. When we grow past the point of creating for ourselves, we grow into creating for the good of the community.

But, regardless of where you're at, if you're growing a vision, that vision will eventually grow beyond just you and you're going to need to bring in some support to help you to achieve the goals.

The biggest problem I see with people at this stage is that they want to surround themselves with people who think and act just like they do. The problem is that the tasks you're going to need accomplished will be more varied than that. You'll want to allocate people to tasks that they're good at.

I equate it to a hockey team, yes because I'm Canadian, and yes because I know more about hockey than other sports. In a hockey team there are usually 6 players on the ice, each holds a different position but each has a different personality too. The centre is not the same personality type as the goalie. They have completely different skill sets; they act, walk and talk completely differently. They even look different. Do they help each other? Always! The forwards are different from the defence, but they're also different from the centre. You need to understand that they're going to have not only different skill set, but they're going to have different attitudes and as such, they're not always

Business Ownership Mindset

going to get along. They don't have to. They don't have to be best buddies with each other all the time. But, they have a shared vision of what they want to do and what they want to accomplish as a team, and they know that they're all in it together.

Now being able to find those personality types that you need in your office, the administration types, or data entry types are going to have a totally different personality than your marketing person or than your sales person. You have to understand that and create a team that's really going to pull together and work together even though they may not necessarily get along.

In other words, you can't create a team in your own image. Five clones of you isn't going to create the synergy you need to create something new beyond what you could have done on your own.

Some people will say that they DO in fact want a clone, someone who does what they do, as well as they do it. But really you don't. Without that unique characteristic added into the office, you're not going to get the creative element that allows you to come up with epiphanies and ideas that go beyond your own perspective.

Now I'm not saying that you have to keep coming up with new ways of doing things or change for the sake of change, but what I am saying is that when people are challenged in a healthy way, debates can spring up, new information can be put on the table and solutions to problems that may not have been solved otherwise can now be solved.

To engage others and respectfully stand your ground allows you to see a whole new way of dealing with things that can simplify, speed up and improve your processes. Or said in another way, can make your business grow stronger, faster, more easily.

Do you as the leader need to create trust in such a diverse group? Yes! Absolutely. Diversity is not commonly accepted in our society yet, sadly enough. In order to bring out the best in your people you're going

Business Ownership Mindset

to have to welcome the conversation, appreciate the charged environment and teach people to bring their strongest talents forward.

When you're gathering together your team, as I mentioned before, you're going to want to put together a list of tasks or project that you want to get done. You're ideally going to group those tasks into personality types and skill sets. You'll do this so that you can more easily find the person who can do that job. In the beginning you might think it's one person, but it might be two completely different people. I know that means you're complicating the relationship factor in your office. It's going to mean more communicating and different communicating, but in the end it'll mean that the jobs get done better and more efficiently than they would have with one person and you're not trying to find a unicorn.

You might even want to ask yourself who else is around you that you need to bring on board? Maybe there's already someone in your life that you think would be perfect for your company, but you don't know how to fit them in. When this happens I find, more often than not, that it was the perfect person to hire. Sometimes that unique perspective allows you to break out of molds that you've built around yourself that you didn't know you made. Don't get me wrong, you still want to do your due diligence and put safeguards in place in case it doesn't work. But, if you allow yourself to open up to possibilities that weren't there before, it might just be that thing you were looking for to get you out of the doldrums.

Business Ownership Mindset

2. <u>Masterminding</u>

Masterminding can be a brilliant way to build your business. If you're not part of a mastermind right now, find one that fits you and join it. Depending on what you bring to the table and what calibre of entrepreneur or Business Owner that you want to interact with, will depend on how you find these people, how you meet and interact and how much it'll cost. Ideally you want to find one where you can help others and they can help you, so you want to be in the middle of the pack, but that won't always be the case.

If you don't know what a mastermind is you might want to read Think and Grow Rich by Napoleon Hill. It's a classic and what I would consider essential reading for every entrepreneur. In his book he refers to a group of people with likeminded intentions. He said, "The mastermind may be defined as: Coordination of knowledge and effort in the spirit of harmony, between two or more people, for the attainment of a definite purpose."

He goes on to say, "No individual may have great power without availing himself of the "Master Mind."

There are so many reasons that people don't have great power without a mastermind, the least of which is that they'll tend to fall back to their path of least resistance, which might be buying into the mindset of the people around them, even if those are well intended good people. If they have an employee mentality, which your staff should have, then you'll especially need a group of entrepreneurs to talk to, to shine light on non-supportive thinking. Hill went on to say, "Deliberately seek the company of people who influence you to think and act for yourself." That is sage advice.

Business Ownership Mindset

3. **Letting Go of Resistance**

I'm pretty sure I've beaten this idea to submission, but in case I haven't; resistance is not fear or trauma or oppression. Resistance is ANY idea or belief that hinders your progress. Saying, "I should really go to the rehearsal instead", can be resistance. Thinking you SHOULD do something instead of knowing what you want to do and why, is resistance. Thinking you NEED to do something. Deciding that cleaning the baseboards is more important than prospecting is resistance. Being nice to someone when you know asking them a tough question would be more powerful in creating a connection that you want is resistance.

Any time you aren't thinking, feeling or doing what you want to in order to get you closer to your goals is resistance. Not making the kind of money that you want to is resistance. Any feeling that keeps popping up whether it's negative or positive that isn't getting you to your goal is resistance. For example going out with your friends because it feels better than doing your accounting that's due tomorrow morning is resistance even though it feels good at the time.

How do you let it go? First you have to recognize that it's there. Write a list of all the thoughts, feelings, actions and results that you're having or getting right now that you don't want or that are moving you away or keeping you away from your goals.

Once you have that list, figure how you want to let go of them. Some are going to be simple. You're just going to look at it once it's on paper, realize that you don't really believe that any more and that it's time to let it go. If you can, do that all day long with everything that doesn't work for you.

Some items on your list are going to be a little more ingrained. Some of them, you might even think that's just the way it is, that's who I am or that everyone does that. That may be true, but I doubt it. Yes

Business Ownership Mindset

people get angry, but not everyone holds on to it. Yes it's normal to cry at certain situations, but it doesn't mean you have to. Looking deeper into the things that hold you back from being you will help you to decipher if things are law or conditioning.

If it's law, it's true for everyone all of the time and it always has been. Gravity is true for everyone all the time and it always will be. Step off the planet and the laws of gravity still exist, you just experience them differently based on your proximity to large mass.

Conditioning on the other hand is not true for everyone all the time. Crying at a funeral is conditioning. Some people do it some people don't. Fear of rejection is conditioning. Some people experience it and some people don't. Need for approval is conditioning, some people need it and some people don't. It doesn't mean you're not human if you experience these things and it doesn't mean you're not human if you don't experience these things. Emotions like approval and rejection are normal human emotions that everyone will experience at some point, but it doesn't mean they have to. Therefore, it's just conditioning. The good news is that if it's just conditioning, then you can change it!

If you're experiencing something that, up until now you thought was "just the way it is" then it's vital that you know that isn't true. It's not. And just because you may not have found a way to change it up until now doesn't mean it can't be changed.

With Success Therapy we change a tremendous amount of conditioning that people thought, that's just the way it was. So, if you haven't found your solutions yet, please give us a call and discuss the possibilities with you. We've created tremendous changes in people's lives from nail biting to PTSD and we can certainly help with business related resistance.

People will often come to me for business coaching and within short order they start to realize that their business related resistance is

Business Ownership Mindset

not only the cause of their work related issues but also their stress and health related issues. I personally tie them all together and don't see the separation, but I'm learning that not everyone sees it that way.

The way I see it, our body is in a constant state of flow; blood flows, fluid flows, everything is in constant motion. When we hold on to an idea or an emotion we slow or even stop that flow. Emotionally we call it "holding on" to something. Physically we'll call it a tightening or a block. When we hold on to an emotion and don't express it or release it, eventually will create tightening or a block in the body, whether it's muscular or nervous. If we continue to hold on to that tightening or block for long enough eventually the muscle or nerves can't heal as fast as the break down and the muscle or nerve begins to break down physically and then visibly.

That whole process to me is simply the way we function as humans and it's not separated into work or personal or otherwise, it's simply a function of the whole.

To reverse that process, you need to give yourself permission to express, and that all starts with figuring out what's not being expressed, which takes us to the top of the section where I suggested you write a list of all the thoughts, feelings, actions and results that you're having or getting right now that you don't want or that are moving you away or keeping you away from your goals.

Business Ownership Mindset

4. <u>**Coaching**</u>

If you want to be a professional master of anything you need a coach. I don't care if it's playing basketball or selling online computer parts. If you want to make serious money at it and be one of the best around, you need a coach. And, maybe you're already the best around. You still need a coach to keep you there.

There's a huge difference between a coach, a mentor and a mastermind. Your mastermind is there to help you brainstorm, share best practices and encourage you. Your mentor is there is to tell you what they're doing and how to make it work. Your coach is there to pull the best out of you, get you to the point of making a decision, hold you accountable to those decisions and to give you an anal cranialectomy when you need one. If you don't have a love/hate relationship with your coach, they're not coaching you, they're coddling you. If they're coddling you they might be a good accountability partner or cheerleader, but they're not coaching you.

I know most coaching programs teach their coaches how to ask questions of you their client, which is great. But you need to find a coach that does more than that. Reading a book will get you to do that. Find someone that calls you on your crap, makes you dig a little deeper and see things in a more expansive way.

Remember I don't think you're in business for people to go, "Raw, raw! Sis boom ba! You're the greatest!" You're here to see what you're made of! Yes, of course I start every coaching call with, "What's going right?" because you need to train your brain for success. You need to be able to see success everywhere and train your brain that's the way you are. You're a magic making machine! I get it! Yay! Ya, you're a rockstar! Ya, you're amazing. We celebrated. Now what are you going to do? You want to constantly be looking at what's slowing you down and get it out

Business Ownership Mindset

of your way.

I heard it best in To Kill a Mocking Bird when the father says to Scout, "Childhood is what you spend the rest of your life trying to overcome." I believe that to be true in every sense of the words. I believe the reason we live so intensely as children is so that we absorb everything we can in those formidable years, taking in every thread of thought that we possibly can and then we spend the rest of our time unravelling the knots and reweaving the tapestry of our lives.

If we want to do it to the best of our ability then we're going to need help. You don't want someone who necessarily knows your job, that's what a mentor is for, you want someone who knows you, who can pull the best out of you.

Business Ownership Mindset

Chapter 17
Conclusion

1. Review Highlights

You know what? I'm going to leave this blank for you. I was going to fill it in, but now that I'm here, I'm thinking you can write in here the main highlights of the book concepts you want to integrate into your life and ideas that are most important to you. The next page is for your to-do's and the following page will be for your follow up notes a year from now.

You really do want to write things here, because a year from now you're going to be blown away by how far you've come in your thinking and in your results.

Business Ownership Mindset

2. **<u>Now Go Do it</u>**

In case you're still really curious about GSD... It's a time in the calendar that I get some of my clients to do when they have odd's and sod's that need to get completed but it keeps falling through the cracks. It's called Get Shit Done. One of my clients even bought me a shirt with that on it. I wear it with pride. Of course, treat everything you do with pride. Think of it more like fertilizer that feeds your business. GFD? Well you get the idea.

Your life is important. This means that your goals are important. Make sure you're writing out your tasks, you know what you're working on next, you know what you want help with should the opportunity to ask someone present itself and you know when it's time to hustle.

Book it in your calendar and get it done.

Business Ownership Mindset

3. **Come Back in a Month and Do it Again.**

You know that your Strategy Meetings are important and your Planning Meetings are important too. Every month you want to be reassessing where you are and verifying that you're on track. Some goals will be monitored daily, maybe, but others might not be reviewed for months if you let them.

If you look back at this on a monthly basis you'll find yourself right on track for those 7 figure and 8 figure projections. Staying true to yourself, willing to let go of resistance, and moving up to the next project on the plan, you will achieve your goals.

Business Ownership Mindset

The hypothesis of a thesis

What if the path to enlightenment was found through running your own company?

Ok, you might not be Buddhist. I'm not. But, what if meaning, fulfilment, purpose and self-actualization were found through owning and running your own company?

What if every fear you ever felt, every heart string that was ever pulled, every spontaneous nudge you ever felt, was pulling you toward going out, starting your own company and building an empire and a legacy?

What if all you had to do was to fan the embers of desire? Here's a toast! To you! From smoldering embers to Earth shaking Kaboom!

Made in the USA
Columbia, SC
16 January 2018